ALL CHANGE & Other Plays

Wolfgang Bauer, born in 1941, belon[...]
remarkably talented Austrian writers
Handke) who came to prominence in th[...]
are widely produced and highly regard[...]
Germany.

Bauer shares with his contemporaries a devastating,
iconoclastic determination to break with the past; his whole
oeuvre must be considered an assault against the traditional
theatre, as well as the audience that attends it. And yet in
its outward form Bauer's writing (unlike Handke's) is not
only realistic but ultra-realistic. American comic books,
Beatle records, English and American detective stories
are the materials of the bored, disillusioned generation he
both represents and portrays. The empty boredom of Magic
Afternoon, which explodes in sudden hatred and violence,
resembles the mood of Waiting for Godot, which it trans-
poses from the stylised expressionist symbolism of Beckett
to the coarse neo-realism of pop art; and like Beckett's
masterpiece it is, ultimately, the reverse of a cry of despair
- an impassioned plea for the courage to face the world as
it is. And, similarly, in the brutal game of manipulation
and counter-manipulation in All Change we can discern a
deeply-felt appeal for the exercise of human freedom.

Wolfgang Bauer lives in Graz, Austria, where he was born
in 1941. He has studied theatre, law, philosophy and
literature, and has written poetry, short stories, plays and
a novel, all of which have been published to critical acclaim
in the German-speaking countries. His short play Film und
Frau was presented as Shakespeare the Sadist by Inter-Action
at The Almost Free Theatre, London, in 1972.

All Change and Party for Six have been translated by Renata
and Martin Esslin. Mr. Esslin is the head of BBC Radio
Drama, the author of standard works on Brecht and The
Theatre of the Absurd and, together with his wife, has translated several plays from the German. Magic Afternoon is
translated by Herb Greer, whose own play, Po' Miss Julie,
was recently seen at the Hampstead Theatre Club.

PLAYSCRIPT 56

'all change' & other plays

PARTY FOR SIX
MAGIC AFTERNOON

wolfgang bauer

TRANSLATED BY MARTIN & RENATA
ESSLIN, HERB GREER

CALDER AND BOYARS · LONDON

First published in West Germany
by Verlag Kiepenheuer & Witsch
Cologne West Germany

(c) Verlag Kiepenheuer & Witsch 1969

These translations first published in Great Britain
by Calder & Boyars Ltd
18 Brewer Street London W1

(c) Calder & Boyars 1973

ISBN 0 7145 0945 0 Cloth Edition
ISBN 0 7145 0946 9 Paper Edition

Printed in Great Britian by
Biddles Ltd, Guildford

CONTENTS

ALL CHANGE

CHARACTERS

AIR VICE MARSHAL   CHARLES DE MARLIMONT
LADY DE MARLIMONT

GEORGIE

FRANK

BASIL

RICHARDS

AMANDA

SONIA

SUZANNE

ANTOINE

1ST PATIENT

2ND PATIENT

MIDDLETON

NURSE PEGGY

DOCTOR

NURSES

SCENE ONE

(The Curtain rises. The stage remains in darkness.
AIR VICE MARSHAL SIR CHARLES DE MARLIMONT's
voice is heard from some way off, the next room but
one)

DE MARLIMONT. The Pope!...That devil, the Pope! The
Pope! (Pause) A whore! You whore, you! Tart! A
common tart!

(LADY DE MARLIMONT's calming voice is heard but
her actual words cannot be distinguished. A key is
turned, footsteps, lights. We see a large kitchen,
with all modern fittings and labour saving devices.
There are two doors: one to the Hall, the second to
GEORGIE's room. GEORGIE enters followed by
FRANK. GEORGIE tosses her white raincoat into a
corner)

LADY DE M. (calling) Is that youououou?

GEORGIE. (mimicking her) Yyyyeeeees!

LADY DE M. Are you aloooooone?

GEORGIE. (smiling at FRANK) Noooo!

(LADY DE MARLIMONT enters. She looks tired and
is careless about her appearance. She wears glasses
and an orange-brown coloured dressing gown)

LADY DE M. Do you have to come home so late?

9

GEORGIE. Go on, don't run around looking like that...
 (She gestures her to leave the room)

LADY DE M. Daddy is in a bad way again.

GEORGIE. Is he.

LADY DE M. No peace! I can't get any peace and quiet!
 Where have you been all this time?

FRANK. Well, first we went to a movie -

GEORGIE. For Christ's sake, don't talk to her!

LADY DE M. You two get married or else part company!
 This to-ing and fro-ing all the time is giving me bad
 turns. (To FRANK) After all, you must know one day
 what you want!

GEORGIE. Go on, creep out of here. What do you look like!

LADY DE M. Surely, in my own house...well, really, that's
 the limit!

GEORGIE. (breaking in) Come on, luvey. (Pushes her out
 through the door) Let's go. Go to your beddie-byes!

LADY DE M. Just you wait!

 (Distant voice: The Pope! That devil, the Pope! You
 whore, you! Bitch! Tart!)

FRANK. You don't have to treat her quite so cruelly, do
 you.

GEORGIE. She drives me crazy, the way she mooches about.
 She'll keep coming in here, you know how she does:
 are you aloooooone? Is that youoououou? Where have
 you been all this time? And she sings every sentence
 as if she was doing a solo in a musical, she's quite
 capable of staying in here and performing her entire
 repertoire of ancient musical numbers.

FRANK. Okay, okay. Give it a rest. I think she's quite
 sweet.

10

GEORGIE. Sweet, my God! When you've got to listen to
her day in, day out... (Lights a cigarette) Are you
going home?

FRANK. I don't know. Do you want me to?

GEORGIE. It's up to you. I'm going to sleep in the kitchen
again.

FRANK. What for?

GEORGIE. Do you think I'm going to listen to him raving
night after night?

FRANK. The Pope?

GEORGIE. Whore! You whore, you! (Goes into her room)

FRANK. The movie was pretty good, wasn't it luv? The
story wasn't much, but the shots were fabulous...
the shots of the actual racing, the Monte Carlo ones
...and the ones at Spa...the whole thing, Monza too,
don't you think? I wouldn't mind seeing it all again.

(GEORGIE enters with bedclothes and drops them on
the floor)

GEORGIE. No chance.

FRANK. Monte Carlo isn't really as good as it looked...
Are you going to kip on the floor?

GEORGIE. How about the sink? Get the record player,
please.

(FRANK goes into her room)

And something to read -

FRANK. What?

GEORGIE. The latest number of JETSET, with that piece
about the College of Fun. I haven't read it yet.

(FRANK tosses a magazine through the door. GEORGIE opens the fridge and helps herself to some yogurt. FRANK brings in the record player)

FRANK. Can you plug it in here? Oh yeah... (Puts it down) Listen, I think I'll stay.

GEORGIE. You'd better go home.

FRANK. Got any beer? Shall we open a can?

(GEORGIE hands him a can of beer. FRANK puts on some soft music, opens can and pours. Doorbell)

GEORGIE. Who's that?

FRANK. Better go and see before the old bitch starts up her song and dance again.

(GEORGIE goes to the door. Voices. LADY DE MARLIMONT's voice:)

LADY DE M. (off) Georgieieie? Who is it? Georgie, daaarling, who is it?

GEORGIE. It's for me. Stay where you are.

LADY DE M. (off) Who is it?

GEORGIE. For me! (Softly) Come inside, quick.

(BASIL, RICHARDS and GEORGIE make a dash for the kitchen)

RICHARDS. How do you do, my lord and master.

FRANK. How are things?

BASIL. (introducing himself) My name is Basil O'Malley.

RICHARDS. Not too bad. Just happened to be passing...
Mr. O'Malley wanted to meet you, or rather I
wanted you to meet Mr. O'Malley. He is also a painter
(Winks at FRANK) Actually at present he is a lock-

smith by trade, but he wants to be a painter. A man with a future you might say.

FRANK. Well, sit down. Or lie down.

RICHARDS. Are you two sleeping in the kitchen?

GEORGIE. I am. (An artificial laugh) He is imagining things again. (Points at FRANK)

RICHARDS. Excessive imagination is never a good thing.

GEORGIE. You're not kidding.

FRANK. So what! If you think you're getting a drink you're wrong.

RICHARDS. Good Lord, no, what do you mean, we're just dropping in.

(BASIL is looking through his folder and picks out one or two of his works, muttering 'hhmm'. RICHARDS points to him)

RICHARDS. (to FRANK) Well, wouldn't you like to ask Mr. O'Malley what he has got in his folder?

FRANK. Does he always carry all his work around with him?

(RICHARDS smiles in the affirmative)

May one have a look?

BASIL. (looking up) I don't know whether you are sufficiently interested in my work.

FRANK. Sufficiently interested, he says.

RICHARDS. Of course our Frankie's interested, aren't you?

(BASIL chooses a picture. RICHARDS indicates to FRANK: The greatest dabbler in Christendom)

13

Is there enough light?

BASIL. (looking around) I think it will do. (Shows the picture) "Cedar trees at Potters Bar".

FRANK. Cedar trees at Potters Bar.

BASIL. This is one of my early works...this one is better: (Shows the picture) "Cedar Trees at Potters Bar". As you see I have chosen another aspect here.

RICHARDS. There are two sides to everything. (Laughs)

FRANK. Very good...very realistic...

BASIL. (holding up another picture) "Oak tree two miles from Potters Bar".

RICHARDS. Look at that shrub, Frank, there at the back. Doesn't it grab you?

FRANK. (laughing) Fabulous, Georgie, don't you think?

GEORGIE. Yes, very nice, why shouldn't it be?

RICHARDS. (serious) We didn't say it wasn't.

BASIL. (takes another sketch) This one isn't too...but this one: "Group of elm trees three miles from Potters Bar". In the left background you can see my bike - it's a Norton Commander.

RICHARDS. Oh yes, - most important.

FRANK. Looks really quite aesthetic.

BASIL. (another picture) "Trees, trees, trees - and where is Potters Bar?"

FRANK. Is that the title?

BASIL. It is.

RICHARDS. Where the hell is Potters Bar? I can't see

anything but trees.

BASIL. Look closely.

GEORGIE. There!

RICHARDS. You don't say! There's a chimney.

FRANK. Splendid. Just like picture puzzles. You could send them to a magazine for a puzzle competition.

RICHARDS. I don't know if our maestro here would agree to that, eh?

(BASIL smiles, embarrassed)

FRANK. What made you take up painting? Did you start all on your own?

BASIL. No, I wouldn't say that...I suddenly felt I had to paint!

FRANK. That has been known to happen. (To RICHARDS) Wouldn't you agree, Hugh? It has been known to happen! (Grins)

RICHARDS. The muse seduced him with her iron grip... (Chuckles)

FRANK. (solemn) Paint beautiful trees! She crooned into his ear! (Laughs)

GEORGIE. Christ, how childish can you get!

(BASIL smiles at her)

FRANK. Do you paint anything else but trees?

RICHARDS. Every artist has his hang-up, and with him it's trees. (Laughs)

FRANK. It's really amazing how much is happening amongst the younger generation.

(BASIL ties his folder)

RICHARDS. Let's go somewhere.

BASIL. How about Ronnie's Place?

FRANK. He knows his way around, doesn't he.

GEORGIE. You can go. I'm going to bed.

FRANK. Do you have to go right now?

GEORGIE. You run along with them!

RICHARDS. At least we should get something to drink.

BASIL. That's true. I'm all for it.

RICHARDS. You get us something, Basil.

BASIL. I don't mind. Where from? What do you want?

RICHARDS. (looks around) What shall we have?

GEORGIE. Nothing as far as I am concerned.

FRANK. Couldn't care less.

RICHARDS. Well, let's have a drop of Champers, shall we,
    by way of celebration?

FRANK. Okay.

GEORGIE. Okay did you say? Don't make me laugh. You're
    not going out to get some champagne, are you?

RICHARDS. (to BASIL) It's quite simple. You go out of
    the front door, turn right at the corner, and fifty
    yards up on the left you'll see a place called "Club 77".
    That's it.

GEORGIE. Will it still be open?

FRANK. Till four in the morning. Give him the key.

BASIL. See you later then!

(GEORGIE goes into the room next door)

RICHARDS. Well, what do you think?

FRANK. He's great, that boy.

RICHARDS. Isn't he just.

FRANK. A real gem.

RICHARDS. Since we are in the kitchen...is there anything to eat?

FRANK. Hey, Georgie. Could you get Mr. Richards a sandwich or something?

GEORGIE. Okay.

FRANK. What are you doing in there?

GEORGIE. Nothing.

RICHARDS. That chap O'Malley turns up at my local day after day...always with his folder, with his pictures...

FRANK. Waiting to pounce —

RICHARDS. Waiting to pounce. And when a victim comes along (Laughs) he pushes his trees under his nose. One wood after another.

FRANK. No.

RICHARDS. And do you know where he comes from? Potters Bar.

FRANK. I might have known.

RICHARDS. He's really a locksmith, I told you, didn't I. He just dabbles with paints in his spare time. The most ridiculous amateur I've ever come across. And in the evening he tries to lead a great social life.

(Laughs loudly) He rides into Town on his bike, his Norton Commander please note, and turns up at my local to meet genuine artists. (Laughs) A regular double existence! A little double faced Janus head from suburbia.

(Distant: The Pope... The Pope!)

What's that? The Pope? Someone wants the Pope?

FRANK. That's her father.

RICHARDS. (pointing to his forehead) He's a bit... how awful...

(Distant: The Pope!)

FRANK. He's great...

RICHARDS. Has he got a political thing or something?

FRANK. Sure. He's only got two things on his mind: either the Pope or he is insanely jealous. He lives under a constant delusion that the old bitch is deceiving him, the dear old Air Vice Marshal!

RICHARDS. Maybe she is?

FRANK. Go on.

GEORGIE. (enters in a mini nightdress) What do you want to eat?

RICHARDS. What? Well, something, anything you've got. I don't want to put you out but, I was just saying, since we are going to camp out in the kitchen anyw...

GEORGIE. I've got three eggs...

RICHARDS. Yes, please. (Smiling at FRANK) Two eggs will be fine.

(GEORGIE sets about preparing the food, at the same time making more noise than necessary)

18

FRANK. (looking through BASIL's folder) One really should try to arrange an exhibition with all this.

RICHARDS. Yes, Pop from Potters Bar or something like that.

FRANK. You could write something about him in your paper, some blown-up interpretation of his tree plantations...?

RICHARDS. One might turn him into some minor Douanier Rousseau...the Customs Officer from Potters Bar! His technique's good. At least I'll say that for him.

FRANK. Or you could build him up into some great artistic personality.

RICHARDS. How do you mean?

FRANK. Don't you see, what I mean...I mean, one could build him up...

RICHARDS. Manipulated man. (Laughs)

FRANK. Right.

GEORGIE. You should be getting on with your work, not talking about manipulating.

FRANK. You know, so that you can say: This is a manipulation by Frank Swann! Not bad, eh?

RICHARDS. And then you stage a gigantic private view where you exhibit him like...a pedigree poodle at a dog show.

FRANK. Make a big star out of him.

RICHARDS. That's not very likely. (To GEORGIE) Ah, the eggs are turning...

FRANK. You'd have to loosen him up a bit first -

GEORGIE. Hahaha!

RICHARDS. Oh, I don't know.

FRANK. One should guide him so that he will simply do everything you tell him. For instance, kill himself. Everything around him should be... organised in such a way, that he can't do anything but kill himself.

RICHARDS. (taking the egg dish from GEORGIE) Thank you. (To FRANK) Why go that far? (To GEORGIE) These artists are real sadists.

FRANK. Sadists...that reminds me. Can you let me have some bread until the day after tomorrow? (Laughs)

RICHARDS. How much?

FRANK. A fiver will do.

RICHARDS. (with deliberate generosity) First I want to eat this.

FRANK. What do I get if I turn Basil into a real painter?

RICHARDS. (to GEORGIE) He can't get it out of his head!

FRANK. Well, what do I get?

RICHARDS. If he kills himself - a thousand quid.

GEORGIE. Food okay?

RICHARDS. Yes, fine thanks. I hope he won't be long with the champers.

FRANK. Wouldn't that be the most accomplished murder of all times? Eh? What do you think?

GEORGIE. Very funny!

(Footsteps in the Hall)

RICHARDS. I'm not too keen on the murder angle. But you're right, one might be able to turn that chap into something. The absurd thing about the art world is that, with a bit of promotion, I might well be able to sell our dear old Basil O'Malley.

FRANK. I'll bet you can.

RICHARDS. He is technically perfect, every leaf looks like a photograph. (Eating) Well, I don't suppose anyone will run after his greenery. But suppose he learns to draw people as well as trees. Or at least himself. "Basil O'Malley in a Cedar Wood"...or how about "Basil and a conifer"! (Laughs)

FRANK. That's what I mean. Not bad material, d'you see. To me he is like a canvas, an empty canvas...

RICHARDS. A canvas! (Laughs)

FRANK. And I am going to paint on it. That'll be something interesting for a change. But not with a brush and paints...(Painting gesture) wishywashy...dot, dot, comma, dash, and you've got your face...popart or informal...all rubbish...all shit...no go. O'Malley will have to be manipulated in his entirety...that is total art...but you'll have to help...

RICHARDS. You're becoming fanatic...

GEORGIE. His mind's going.

FRANK. Shut up. It fascinates me. At last here's something that really excites me. I suddenly feel enormously productive!

RICHARDS. Only you won't get any bread out of it.

GEORGIE. Right. You tell him that!

FRANK. To hell with bread...Oh yes, that Fiver you promised me.

RICHARDS. (has finished eating) Okay. (Takes out his wallet) I've only got three singles, I can hardly give you a ten quid note.

FRANK. Thanks. That's big of you.

LADY DE M. You really must call it a day now, it's one
o'clock!

(The lavatory door is opened and closed)

GEORGIE. All right, all right, go to bed!

(She puts on a record, softly, turns on a small lamp
and turns off the centre light)

(To FRANK) Open the window a bit.

(FRANK opens the window and looks out)

FRANK. Can't see him anywhere.

(GEORGIE also looks out. The AIR VICE MARSHAL
appears in the doorway in semi-darkness, his head
bandaged. He stands and it is sometime before
RICHARDS notices him)

RICHARDS. (suspicious) Good evening, sir.

(GEORGIE quickly turns and utters a short cry)

DE MARLIMONT. (in a broken voice) Ah, there are the
gentlemen...there...there...in the kitchen...a
brothel in the kitchen...where is she...where is
she? Where is that whore? Where is the bitch!
(Shakes RICHARDS)

GEORGIE. Mummy! It's Daddy! Mummy!

LADY DE M. I'm in the loo!

DE MARLIMONT. Where is she? Where? Where is the
whore? (He begins to take crockery from the cup-
boards and smashes it) The Pope...(Murmurs)
the Pope...Where is she fucking, the old bitch?
Where? Where!? Where?

GEORGIE. Mummy loves only you.

DE MARLIMONT. Rubbish, lies.

(LADY DE MARLIMONT rushes in)

LADY DE M. Come along, Charles...

DE MARLIMONT. (points to RICHARDS who is smiling at
  FRANK) Who is that?

(LADY DE MARLIMONT pushes him out of the kitchen)

DE MARLIMONT. Who is that? (He is pushed outside)
  Who is that gentleman...

LADY DE M. Come along, dear, off you go.

(She closes the door to his room and turns the key. He
bangs against the door. She returns to the kitchen)

That's settled it. You'll have to go.

GEORGIE. But we're getting champagne.

LADY DE M. Never mind. I want to get some peace...

GEORGIE. But Mummy...

LADY DE M. No but Mummy...off you go...please! (To
  RICHARDS) You might show a bit of sense, you look
  a little more grown up...

RICHARDS. (rising) Are you coming?

LADY DE M. Of course he's coming.

FRANK. Okay. (Kissing GEORGIE lightly on the cheek)
  See you.

RICHARDS. Bye now.

FRANK. Give me a ring tomorrow.

LADY DE M. (in the kitchen) As if one didn't have enough
  troubles! You're turning night into day and day into

night. And then you sleep all day.

GEORGIE. Go on, scram.

LADY DE M. Either you get yourself a job next month or
you can pack your bags...

GEORGIE. Go on...

LADY DE M. I mean it, this time.

GEORGIE. Then you burst into floods of tears and ring
everybody up to find out where I am. Look, why don't
you leave me alone?

LADY DE M. When I was your age I was appearing at the
Opera House in Blackpool as Principal Boy. I had my
own car, bought with my own earnings! You're nothing
but a layabout, and with your father in such a bad way.

GEORGIE. He's only in such a bad way because you've
always treated him badly...as if he was dirt...

LADY DE M. (screams) That is not true!

GEORGIE. (laughs) Why are you screaming then?

LADY DE M. Because it is not true!

GEORGIE. Don't get excited or your heart will play you up
again.

LADY DE M. Just you wait, the good Lord will punish you!

GEORGIE. Don't be such a hypocrite! (Screams) You're
only waiting for him to kick the bucket. You're praying
for it!

LADY DE M. You wicked bitch you, if I tell Daddy that...
you wicked... (Slaps her face)

(GEORGIE hits back. They pull each other's hair.
GEORGIE pushes her mother out of the door and slams
it)

GEORGIE. Bloody fool!

(She puts on a record, turns it up loud and sings in a
loud voice. A loud whistle outside, she goes to the
window, runs to the record player, turns it off and
hurries back to the window)

Where have you been all this time?

BASIL. They wouldn't serve me. I went on to Ronnie's
Place.

GEORGIE. Everyone's gone.

BASIL. I've got a bottle of Vodka. I'll bring it up!

GEORGIE. Okay. (She goes to the door)

BASIL. (enters) Got any glasses?

GEORGIE. Hang on, hang on. (Takes two glasses)

(BASIL puts on record, pours. They drink. BASIL
begins to laugh)

What are you laughing about?

BASIL. (pours some more) We could make beautiful music
together!

(The drink. He throws himself onto the bed clothes
on the floor, whistles to the record. GEORGIE
closes the window, walks slowly round BASIL lying
on the floor)

SCENE TWO

(A Boutique "ADAM AND EVE". Darkness on stage.
BASIL's motorcycle, a Norton Commander, is heard
approaching. It stops. Footsteps. Someone tries to
open a lock. Sound of scratching and a chisel.

Attempts to open the lock. Hammering. Knocking.
Gentle pulling to and fro of the door for some time.
The door opens, footsteps on stage in the stockroom
and the boutique)

BASIL. I'd like to know where the light is.

(Light. BASIL looks around with pleasure)

Come on in! Come on! I wouldn't stop outside.

GEORGIE. You're out of your mind, Basil!

BASIL. What, me? Why should I be out of my mind?

GEORGIE. Turning the light on.

BASIL. Can't see otherwise.

GEORGIE. Breaking in like that! You're mad.

BASIL. After all, I am a fully trained locksmith.

GEORGIE. What if someone comes?

BASIL. Who should come? It's not exactly main shopping
hours just now, is it? Four o'clock in the morning.
Just the right time of day for shopping.

GEORGIE. Shopping, that's rich!

BASIL. Did you say I was to get myself some new clothes,
or didn't you?

GEORGIE. Yes, but I didn't mean it like this. Let's go.

BASIL. You're dead right, I need some new gear. I'm
going to stay in Town from now on. A painter of my
stature has to be trendy. There are some really
fabulous things in here. (Looks around) You choose
something too!

GEORGIE. You first. I'll tell you if it fits you.

BASIL. What do you mean, fits... (Tries on a jacket and
holds a brightly coloured shirt against it) Pretty cool,
eh?

GEORGIE. (shyly picks out some green trousers) These go
with it. (Studying him) Very discreet.

BASIL. (shocked) Discreet?

GEORGIE. (laughing) No, of course not. (Noticing a cap)
Try this one! Fabulous! That's great...

(BASIL admires himself in a mirror)

BASIL. Beautiful! I look really beautiful...

GEORGIE. Yes - yes, you do!

BASIL. You get yourself something.

GEORGIE. I'm scared.

BASIL. Rubbish, nothing's going to go wrong for me today.
I feel it deep inside me...I feel really good! You
know, pussycat, there are times when I feel really
good!

GEORGIE. (trying on a midi skirt) Look.

BASIL. We'll buy it.

(They look around trying things on)

GEORGIE. (aside) Tell me, are you really that keen on me?

BASIL. I'm keen on everything. How do you like this tie?

GEORGIE. Yeah, very nice... Tell me, are you really that
keen on me?

BASIL. How do you mean 'that keen'?

GEORGIE. I'm only asking.

(Pause.   They try on clothes)

BASIL.   You mean because I've been saying 'I love you' all
the time?

GEORGIE.   Look, does that fit?

BASIL.   No.   Because I've been saying it?

GEORGIE.   That's one of the reasons.

BASIL.   (puts on jacket and dances in front of the mirror) I
love you! I love you! I love you! (Points his tongue)
Do you know what that means?

GEORGIE.   No.   (Tossing a dress aside)

BASIL.   It's like saying 'How do you do' 'How do you do'
'How do you do' or 'Good morning' 'Good evening' or
'Oh dear' or 'how very nice', 'very nice', 'very nice'.
It's just something you say.

GEORGIE.   I can't figure you out.

BASIL.   What you say is immaterial, the main thing is what
you experience. You can experience more in one day
than others in their whole lifetime. (Puts on a bath-
robe) You've got to grab happiness greedily like an
octopus! Uuuuuuueeeeeeh!

(He moves towards her with the movements of an
octopus, she withdraws in surprise, giggling, finally
he embraces her with his tentacles)

Uuuuuueeeeeeh!

(She escapes him, he circles round her slowly, be-
witching her, making sounds of Uuuuuueeeeeeh)

GEORGIE.   Don't make so much noise!

(BASIL makes louder noises)

For God's sake be quiet!

28

(He throws her onto the clothes, dances round her, growing softer, making loving sounds, bends over her, chirps like a bird, tickles her. His appearance is threatening, unpredictable and amusing)

BASIL. "I love you'." (Tickles her) Uuuuuueeeeeh'.

(Chirps. Pokes a finger into her stomach. An alarm is heard)

GEORGIE. What's that?

BASIL. The alarm. Quick, let's get out of here'. (He picks up as many of the clothes as he can grip)

GEORGIE. Leave them'.

BASIL. You take some too.

GEORGIE. Leave them, you fool'.

(Tries to pull the clothes away from him)

BASIL. Shut up'.

GEORGIE. (tugging at his clothes) Leave them'. (Screams) You're mad'.

BASIL. (throws the clothes on the floor and brutally hits out at GEORGIE) Fuck off'. (He picks up the clothes, runs outside, starts up his motor cycle and rides off).

CURTAIN

SCENE THREE

(FRANK's studio. Early morning sunlight. FRANK and RICHARDS look tired, not having been to bed the night before. But they are enthusiastic about their plan. Soft background music. RICHARDS is sitting at a table making notes which seem to both amuse and

29

fascinate him. FRANK is walking up and down. They sip Coca Cola)

RICHARDS. (looking out of the window) I wish I knew how many nights I've wasted like this.

FRANK. (with enthusiasm) It's going to be gigantic, the greatest enterprise ever! Just imagine it - when we've got him where we want him...when he's really made it ...doinggg.' we drop him and the reverse mechanism starts up. D'you see? That is to say (a) end of success, I mean lack of success professionally, - and then (b) the private mess. That will of course have to be pre-pared during his successful period, consisting of two aspects: first love, second chemistry, that means drugs. In concrete terms: unlucky in love...the bird will really have to wear him down. That means she must have a hold over him and at the same time deceive him, intentionally. Everything will have to be carried out with intent and purpose. And then the withdrawal of drugs...do you follow?

RICHARDS. Yes.

FRANK. You'll smash him to pieces in your various papers... we'll influence prospective buyers and collectors in a negative way, that shouldn't be difficult. Antoine, for instance, will have to be a key figure in this...both as a buyer of pictures and as a pusher of drugs. I'm sure Antoine will join in, I know the way his mind works, the perverse bastard...he's bored stiff.

RICHARDS. Of course, we'd have to get him to go along with us.

FRANK. That should be a cinch! If necessary Georgie will have to come in on it.

RICHARDS. She won't refuse. (Laughs)

FRANK. Oh well, I think it's all over anyway. I don't really care. We could always start again. (Grins)

30

RICHARDS. You're being very cool about it, aren't you.

FRANK. What do you mean cool? On the contrary...I don't
think Antoine cares for women any more.

RICHARDS. Has he changed horses?

FRANK. Ambidexterous, I think. Listen...Antoine will
push him the stuff, that's important to get things
moving. A gradual start with, say, a bit of hash,
then the hard stuff, then a few hypodermics...opium...
it doesn't matter what...and then, all of a sudden...
nothing...no more to be had. What will he do? He
won't go back to Potters Bar. He'll take to drinking.
(Laughs) He isn't good-looking... no money... no bird
will get hooked on him...zoing, he does away with himself.

RICHARDS. And what do you get out of it?

FRANK. A thousand quid from you. Naturally I shall have
documentary evidence. Everything will be photographed
all the decisive stages in O'Malley's life, including the
corpse. I shall write the book to end all books.

RICHARDS. A lot of painters think of writing books.
(Laughs)

FRANK. Writing...writing is a load of rubbish. I shall
be doing what those writer chaps write on their shitty
bits of paper. I shall actually be doing it. I am
manipulating a real life, don't you see?

RICHARDS. I beg your pardon, but I think, in principle,
you are not doing anything different from what a writer
does. This whole manoeuvre...this murder plot
you're working out seems to me...seems to me nothing
but a kind of...oh, what shall I say...you want to get
something out of your system.

FRANK. For God's sake, don't come that one with me again.

RICHARDS. Your conflict is...forgive me...the fact that
you have got a conflict but can't write poetry. Maybe
that's a bit exaggerated, I admit.

FRANK. What sort of a conflict have I got anyway?

RICHARDS. What a question!

FRANK. Well, tell me! What sort of conflict?

RICHARDS. Well...to start with there is a certain Miss
Georgie...

FRANK. No! (Pause)

RICHARDS. You've tried suicide twice...I don't want to
analyse all this just now...you...

FRANK. That's very good of you. Don't bother to analyse
me, spare yourself the trouble of an analysis! Your
analyses are centred on your own ego...you only see
what you want to see.

RICHARDS. In Basil...if I might make one more point...
in Basil you want to fuse your two main aims.

FRANK. Which are what?

RICHARDS. Success and death. And since you can't manage
to achieve either of them for youself, you want to
come face to face with them on another level altogether.
And that's all there is to it.

FRANK. Thank you very much, Mr. Headshrinker.

RICHARDS. But now for my programme. The positive
side. Look!

FRANK. Let's see.

RICHARDS. Summary: technically I have no complaints
about our 'objet trouvé'...our 'objet trouvé manipulé'.
(Laughs) So there's just the question of the subject
matter...to give me the chance of a suitable interpretation. Seeing he's so involved with trees, there
are quite a few things I could say about that. Oh, you
know...the loneliness of modern man...all these
trees represent people with whom he has no contact,

and so on. You'll have to tell him what to paint. As far as promotion is concerned: I shall put two of his sketches into the paper tomorrow. Influential circles will be informed.

FRANK. What about a private view?

RICHARDS. It's too soon for that. First we might have some little scandals. I would suggest...stripping at some formal occasion...for instance at that Reception the Minister for the Arts is holding. What do you think? That will create quite a ripple...television...

FRANK. First class! That's great!

RICHARDS. Or painting other people's cars...you get minor sentences for that kind of thing. He'll survive those and rise free from the police court like a phoenix from the ashes. Then, of course, there will have to be a private programme of education and indoctrination. Books...

FRANK. I have that in mind as well. You can undermine his confidence and induce a defeatist mood with the help of the right kind of author and philosopher.

RICHARDS. Introduce him to as many people as possible... you know a lot of people...

FRANK. Antoine is the most important.

RICHARDS. Yeah - he might be able to move in with him.

FRANK. I'd rather he stayed with me, then I'd have him under my thumb.

RICHARDS. Fair enough. And we'd have to get him hung up on a nice dollybird.

FRANK. Georgie.

RICHARDS. (eyes him dubiously) You do have a twisted mind! Well...(Pause) Tell me, why shouldn't it be you instead? Us do the whole thing to you, I mean. I know why, you wouldn't strip at a Reception!

(Laughs) (Pause) Well, that's roughly how I see it.

FRANK. (pause) There's no reason why it shouldn't go very well... (Puts on a slow record, walks about)

(RICHARDS stretches)

RICHARDS. Ah well, I'm ready for beddie-byes... Hell, I've got to go to the private view at eleven...

FRANK. What private view is that?

RICHARDS. Oh, some old master... (Reads the invitation) Kenneth Debenham... tut, tut...

FRANK. Relative of Freebody's? (Laughs)

RICHARDS. How do I know... I've got my job to do...

FRANK. D'you want anything to eat?

RICHARDS. Eat? Hm, I think I'll have breakfast at home. After all, I've got a family... Who's that on the record?

FRANK. Don't you know.

RICHARDS. Gerry Mulligan?

FRANK. Right.

RICHARDS. From time to time I like to remember the old ones.

FRANK. I'm turning on to jazz again myself.

RICHARDS. Do you know Joey Smeeton?

FRANK. Yeah...

RICHARDS. He's a specialist on the late 'fifties... got stuck there. One of the greatest jazz experts...

FRANK. Quite a nice guy. I...

RICHARDS. You know...jazz...Jesus, I can remember when I used to do a talk on jazz every week...

FRANK. Those were good days...

RICHARDS. There was something going on then...enormous enthusiasm...the heyday of the avant-garde...

(Doorbell. FRANK goes to open the door. RICHARDS rises, puts on his tie, combs his hair. FRANK enters with GEORGIE)

GEORGIE. Morning.

RICHARDS. Morning.

FRANK. You going?

RICHARDS. Yeah... (Considering what to say)...well, then maestro...we'll leave it like that. I expect I'll meet Antoine at the private view. I can put him in the picture a bit.

FRANK. You do that. Give him my regards.

RICHARDS. Right you are then. (Exit)

FRANK. Bye now.

GEORGIE. See you.

FRANK. How come you're up so early?

GEORGIE. Me?

FRANK. Yes, you.

(GEORGIE laughs)

GEORGIE. It's such a lovely day -

FRANK. I haven't had any sleep at all. We've been working on that manipulation.

GEORGIE. (to herself) The what?...Has Basil been here?

FRANK. No. Why should he? He doesn't know where I
live. I'd like to know, though, where he got to last
night.

GEORGIE. Give me a cig.

(FRANK passes her a cigarette. She gives him a
little kiss)

How are you then?

FRANK. Sleepy...but otherwise okay. That guy Richards!

GEORGIE. What's he been doing all night?

FRANK. He's worked out the master plan for O'Malley.

(Shows her the notes, she puts them back)

But - and this is typical of Hugh - he had to start
talking about my subconscious. He said, I only want
to do the whole thing because I am...

GEORGIE. Because that's what you are like.

FRANK. No, not quite like that. Anyway, it doesn't really
matter.

GEORGIE. (yawning) I'm going to lie down for a bit. (Goes
to settee)...(Pause) You're so stupid...why don't
you ask Richards to put some of your work into the
paper or try and get it sold. You're always broke...
we could get married...

FRANK. Hohohoho...you know very well that would be a
waste of time. Come on, honey, we get on much
better like this. This obsession to get married...it's
...it's some ridiculous fixation you've got. (Shakes
his head, walks about)...Do you want some coffee?

GEORGIE. No...you know very well I don't like coffee!

FRANK. I'd like to know where O'Malley ended up last night.

GEORGIE. (laughs) Would you really like to know?

FRANK. Why, do you know?

GEORGIE. No. (Laughs) (Pause) Ah well, he came back to my place...

FRANK. Back to your place! Why didn't you let me know? You're just playing me up.

GEORGIE. After you'd gone...didn't you bump into him?

FRANK. No...

GEORGIE. He arrived immediately afterwards, along with a bottle of Vodka.

FRANK. And then what?

GEORGIE. We finished it up between us.

FRANK. Well? Give me the lowdown - what's he like? I hardly know him.

GEORGIE. Quite nice, actually.

FRANK. You must have got plastered, if you finished off the whole bottle...

GEORGIE. (shaking her head) Well...maybe...

FRANK. And what else?

GEORGIE. The funniest thing happened this morning.

FRANK. Yes?

GEORGIE. He gets up, gets dressed...

FRANK. So you've finally done it!

GEORGIE. You're round the bend.

FRANK. Well, if he had to get dressed?

GEORGIE. Listen. He says: let's go. I say: Where? He says: get some gear. So I say: You're daft, in the middle of the night?

FRANK. Seems to me you're more than friendly with him.

GEORGIE. What do you expect after a bottle of Vodka!

FRANK. Carry on.

GEORGIE. Do you know where he went?

FRANK. No.

GEORGIE. Guess.

FRANK. Where?

GEORGIE. To the ADAM AND EVE Boutique! He breaks a lock, gets inside, pinches all sorts of tops, pants, shirts...God knows what else.

FRANK. Come off it!

GEORGIE. I swear it!

FRANK. And you went inside with him?

GEORGIE. Yes, it was absolutely fascinating! I thought he'd come round to see you.

FRANK. So that's why you are here.

GEORGIE. I thought you'd be interested.

FRANK. Yes, indeed! (Walks about, to himself) That's good. (To GEORGIE) In any case, you're already included in the plan.

GEORGIE. What do you mean?

FRANK. Well, not quite yet. First he's got to establish himself as a painter. Then you are going to tip the scales.

GEORGIE You don't say!

FRANK. You see, you are going to present the turning point. You are going to change the course of the spaceship (Laughs)...you are going to bring the spaceship back to earth.

GEORGIE. I don't know what you are talking about. And I don't care.

FRANK. A hard landing. So you haven't slept with him yet?

GEORGIE. Don't keep asking such idiotic questions.

FRANK. What do you mean 'keep asking'. It's important - yes or no?

GEORGIE. No! But it wouldn't make any difference if I had.

FRANK. Not in this case. But all in good time, sweetheart.

GEORGIE. (from the sofa) Come here.

FRANK. What?

GEORGIE. Come here.

FRANK. (to himself) Exactly! (Makes a note)

(Doorbell)

(To GEORGIE) Go and open the door, would you?

(GEORGIE goes)

GEORGIE. Okay. (Off) Hi!

BASIL. (off) Hail to thee blushing virgin!

(BASIL enters, gaudily dressed, with GEORGIE)

FRANK. Hello there!

BASIL. Hail to thee, hail! I'm thrilled to bits about your tits! Hahaha! How are you, sir?

FRANK. Don't call me sir. My name is Frank.

BASIL. And mine's Basil.

FRANK. I'm afraid I can't offer you a drink, but - eh, did you have a good night?

GEORGIE. Breaking in...

BASIL. Shopping, you mean! Yes, a stupid affair that. Arose out of necessity, you might say.

FRANK. Great. Cigarette?

BASIL. No thanks. (Takes out a cigar and lights it)

FRANK. I thought you'd gone back to Potters Bar.

BASIL. No, I'm going to stay in Town. There's just the question of where I'm going to live.

FRANK. You can stay with me, if you like.

BASIL. (pleased) Really?

FRANK. But you'll have to get on with your painting. Otherwise it's no fun.

BASIL. (with exaggeration) I shall be a great artist! I shall be indebted to you for evermore.

GEORGIE. Where've you been all this time?

BASIL. Everywhere and nowhere! I've been roaring right across town on her. There's nothing better than racing along on my Norton at 80 miles an hour, along the main roads.

FRANK. At this time of day?

BASIL. Right in the middle of the road, in and out of the
traffic.

(GEORGIE laughs)

Toioioinnnng - lovely day today! I must paint something - I simply must.

FRANK. Be my guest. Help yourself to anything you want,
whenever you like. (Puts his arm around BASIL)
And if you want to know anything, just come and ask
me.

BASIL. Got paper and paints?

FRANK. Over there. Help yourself.

BASIL You mean that?

FRANK. Don't ask silly questions! (To GEORGIE) I can't
even remember the last time I was so keyed up to
start painting.

BASIL. Keyed up isn't the word. I'd like to swallow up the
paper!

(GEORGIE laughs. FRANK laughs)

GEORGIE. What are you going to paint?

BASIL. Peace and quiet!

FRANK. A woodland scene, I suppose...eh? Are you going
to paint a woodland scene?

BASIL. A nude!

FRANK. A nude?

BASIL. A nude...what one generally refers to as a nude
painting.

FRANK. Have you ever painted a nude model?

FRANK. Painted? I've never actually painted one.

FRANK. Do you mean to paint a nude without a model?

BASIL. Basil can paint nudes without models, even in the
dark, if necessary. (He smiles)

(GEORGIE smiles too. FRANK notices her)

FRANK. (to GEORGIE) Pussy, wouldn't you like to sit for
him?

GEORGIE. Are you out of your mind?

FRANK. Look, I'm sure Basil would like it if you sat for
him, eh?

BASIL. Quiet! I must concentrate!

FRANK. (to GEORGIE) Go on, won't you do it?

GEORGIE. Leave me alone.

FRANK. But it's very important that Basil should learn to
paint nudes from live models, sweetheart.
(Playfully pinches her nose)

GEORGIE. Go to hell.

FRANK. What? Don't you want to? Come on...don't make
so much fuss about it. You're not usually so prim...
(Begins to undo her dress) Come on, take that off...

GEORGIE. (slaps his face) You're behaving like a seventeen-
year-old...

FRANK. (pulls off top half of the dress) Look Basil, look
quick...

BASIL. Absolute quiet, please.

GEORGIE. (to FRANK) Bloody idiot!

FRANK. (putting on a soft record) Basil, you tell her to take her clothes off. She's shy with me.

BASIL. (vaguely) What's that?

FRANK. You tell her.

BASIL (stands up, looks at GEORGIE with mock serious-ness) I think you are being too clumsy about this, Frank. It's got to be done very slowly, very gently, d'you see?

(Reaches her, starts to undress her slowly)

Very gently...

(He whistles in tune with the record. GEORGIE stands naked. BASIL sits at the drawing board and starts to sing to the record. FRANK laughs)

CURTAIN

SCENE FOUR

(Sleazy Nightclub. Curtained off partitions in the back-ground. It is fairly quiet. A man comes out from behind the curtains, combs his hair and leaves the club. SONIA is at the bar. AMANDA and SUZANNE are busy behind the curtains. Soft music)

AMANDA. (emerges, straightens her hair) What's wrong, the place is like a morgue tonight.

SONIA. It's Wednesday.

AMANDA. On Wednesdays they all stay at home with their wives.

SONIA. Is that one having another bubbly?

AMANDA. He's not drunk the first half of the bottle. Mean

old git!

VOICES. (from behind curtain) Amanda! Amanda!

AMANDA. Okay...

SONIA. Go to Mr. Rainer, luv, would you. Suzie is with Mr. Hetherington. I'll be along in a minute.

AMANDA. Okay.

VOICE. Suzie. Suzie my love!

AMANDA. Coming...

(BASIL and FRANK enter)

SONIA. (eagerly) Gentlemen!

BASIL. Charmed, I'm sure.

(SONIA whistles)

Is this a bloody football ground or something?

(AMANDA enters)

AMANDA. Good evening, Gentlemen. Shall we all have a drink inside?

FRANK. No thanks. We'll stay here.

SONIA. Would you like a long drink, sir? Whisky?

BASIL. Don't you want to go inside, Frankie?

(FRANK gestures: not enough money)

AMANDA. Step inside, you gorgeous creatures.

BASIL. Hang on a minute, no need to rush things. We'll have a drink first.

FRANK. Two beers.

(AMANDA exits)

SONIA. Work up a bit of courage, eh?

BASIL. Cut out the small talk, auntie, or I'll knock you flat on the counter.

SONIA. You're an impulsive one.

VOICE. Sonia! Sonia!

SONIA. Coming! Cheerie-bye, milksops! (Exit)

BASIL. What are we here for? We can drink beer anywhere.

FRANK. Not in such pleasant surroundings. I like it here. It inspires me in some way. Cheers!

(They drink)

It's a relaxed setting, that's always important. It comes out in our work, you see?

(Giggling from behind the curtain)

BASIL. The giggling of these sub-human creatures turns me over.

FRANK. For Christ's sake, don't use words like sub-humans. You sound like Enoch. You'll have to drop that kind of talk if you want to be a success. We may manage to get you an exhibition in two months' time, okay, but you'll have to watch it, Basil. They'll knock you down just as fast. Above all, remember: be relaxed. Your pictures are too rigid...d'you see what I mean, technically they're good, that's okay, some are amusing, but nothing moves, Basil. All the enthusiasm in the world won't help, you've still got a lot to learn. I'm sorry if I'm becoming didactic but read some Beckett, Molloy for example.

BASIL. Molloy, sounds good.

FRANK. Or Ulysses by Joyce, at least the last few chapters

...or Lawrence Sterne...

BASIL. D'you think these birds won't do anything for free?

FRANK. Or read Civilization by Sir Kenneth Clark, or:
The Painting of Schizophrenics...d'you see. Talent is
fine, and you've got talent, but you won't get anywhere
without some background. You're not stupid...

(AMANDA enters with an empty champagne bottle)

AMANDA. (to BASIL) Gorgeous to look at but so inex-
perienced! (Shows him her tongue)

BASIL. Hideous to look at and so battered about! If I were
you I wouldn't open my mouth so wide. Do you want
everyone to see those black stubs of yours you call
teeth?

AMANDA. (massaging the back of BASIL's neck) You
rough little bear!

BASIL. (to FRANK) This is too much!

(AMANDA goes out with another bottle)

FRANK. Or take jazz, you don't know anything about it.
Albert Ayler, Charlie Mingus, have you ever heard
of them?

BASIL. No.

FRANK. You've got an enormous backlog of culture to catch
up on. It's all very well to be naive, it has its
advantages even in the field of painting, it has its own
fascination, but in the end you're always the one who's
left out in the cold.

BASIL. I'm going in there.

FRANK. Stay here, you haven't got a chance without money,
and anyway I want to talk to you.

BASIL. Listen Frank. I'm your friend.

FRANK. Of course you are.

BASIL. I can stay with you.

FRANK. Of course you can.

BASIL. I've got to tell you something. All this talk is use-
less.

FRANK. But...

BASIL. Listen, the other night I slept with your...what's
her name...

FRANK. Georgie.

BASIL. I've slept with her.

FRANK. (surprised) Oh well, that's okay. I thought you
had...

BASIL. Listen, there's something else. She told me you're
planning something, you want to 'build me up'...

FRANK. Go on...

BASIL. She said that I'd end up killing myself. I didn't
quite get what she meant. Being in the kitchen it was
all a bit odd. But tell me, is it true?

FRANK. It's quite untrue.

BASIL. What did you have in mind, little Picasso? (Pinches
his nose)

(SONIA comes out)

SONIA. Well, make up your mind yet?

BASIL. You think about it'. (To SONIA) Let's go, one
bottle, please.

SONIA. And one for the other gentleman?

BASIL. He's got some thinking to do.

SONIA. Oh, a proper scholar! (Laughs)

(SONIA takes a bottle and disappears behind the curtain with BASIL)

VOICE. Sonia!

BASIL. (off) No Sonia for you, my friend!

(FRANK sits alone, searches for money, puts it on the bar counter. RICHARDS enters)

RICHARDS. A very good evening one and all!

FRANK. Hello Hugh.

RICHARDS. You alone?

FRANK. Basil's in there. (Points to curtains)

RICHARDS. Oh, I see. (Laughs) I suppose he is busy being built up!

FRANK. Well, I think things may turn out harder than we thought.

RICHARDS. He's practising stripping for tomorrow. (Laughs)

FRANK. I don't know.

RICHARDS. What's the matter with you, what's wrong?

FRANK. What should be wrong?

RICHARDS. Feeling all right?

FRANK. Yeah, I'm feeling all right.

RICHARDS. You don't look it though. You look as if you were in one hell of a mess.

FRANK. What do you know about my situation...

RICHARDS. I know, I've said it before; you're always in the situation that <u>you think</u> others think you are in.

(AMANDA comes out. A man leaves)

AMANDA. So long, Mr. Rainer! (To RICHARDS) Hello there, Hugh my love!

RICHARDS Hello there, how are you?

AMANDA. What are you drinking?

RICHARDS. Give me something to settle my stomach... brandy I think.

AMANDA. Is your learned friend having one too?

FRANK. No thanks.

RICHARDS. Give him another beer, Amanda.

AMANDA. Right-ho.

(Excited voices from behind curtain, SONIA and BASIL)

SONIA. Why the hell did you order a bottle if you can't pay for it? Get out!

BASIL. Don't be so practical. Just when it's getting cosy.

SONIA. Get out you git! Get out!

(BASIL appears)

BASIL. What a shambles! Hello Hugh, you drunken sod.

RICHARDS. What's up?

SONIA. He doesn't want to pay for his drink the bastard, the shit!

RICHARDS. How much?

SONIA. Eighty-five bob.

BASIL. You don't think I'm going to pay that much, do you?
You and your black teeth! You ought to count yourselves lucky to be allowed to touch a lovely man like
myself, you slimy toads!

RICHARDS. Silence! (Pays the money) There you are, now
shut up. Come on Basil. (Clicks his fingers) Amanda!
(To FRANK) Coming to celebrate, Frank?

FRANK. Go away and play.

BASIL. (going with RICHARDS) Now they're going to get it!

FRANK. What about my beer.

AMANDA. Coming right up, sir!

CURTAIN

SCENE FIVE

(At ANTOINE's. The room is decorated in velvet
red. Very distinguished. ANTOINE wears a purple
velvet smoking jacket. He is arranging some things
on a small table: ashtrays, hashish cigarettes, a
bowl of punch. A record is playing: Sir John Gielgud
in the Storm Scene from King Lear. Doorbell.
ANTOINE goes to the door and opens)

ANTOINE. (off) Let me embrace you, dearest hedgehog.

FRANK. (off) Hello! Antoine!

(They enter)

ANTOINE. Rest your weary limbs, m'dear. (Arranges

50

cushions) I've been awaiting you eagerly.

FRANK. Yes...well, Georgie and Basil will be here soon.

ANTOINE. Basil...(Giggles) I love that name. And how are you, my dear old friend? (Turns off record)

FRANK. All right, thanks.

ANTOINE. As successful as ever?

FRANK. Well, you know, I'm not doing much work just now.

ANTOINE. Well, I must say your last exhibition was absolutely tops. Absolutely tops. Only yesterday I had a friend of mine here from Paris, Pierre Bauer. I showed him your catalogue. He wants to meet you in the next few days and he says it might well be possible to arrange an exhibition for you in Paris, m'dear. You see, your dear old Antoine does for you what he can.

FRANK. Thanks a lot. But just now I've got my mind on other things, you know what...that's why I'm here.

ANTOINE. Yes. Great! Absolutely first class! When I heard of your diabolical plan...(Pensive) well, I turned a few somersaults inside myself with joy. (Grins like an old woman)

FRANK. Are you with us then?

ANTOINE. Antoine is always with it, because...well because...being with it, being right at the heart of things, is everything. (Giggles) Not just on the edge of things, my dear little hedgehog! (Stares at FRANK, laughs) Right...(Rises) now we'll play our private national anthem.

FRANK. The Pathétique?

ANTOINE. Indeed. (Puts on record) Now tell me all about that rumpus at the Minister's Reception. Did that little rascal really strip?

FRANK. I wasn't there, but it's supposed to have been great. All things considered, the manipulation is going fine - full speed ahead.

ANTOINE. Manipulation - is that what you call it? A real stroke of genius! But tell me, how did you get this - well, you might call it magical idea?

FRANK. It just kind of happened. One thing leads to another. I...you know, it's just an occupation like any other. (Smiling) Only it's nice and pointless.

ANTOINE. (after a little hesitation, affecting seriousness) Frankie, I can only congratulate you. You are one of the last of those favoured beings...

(Doorbell. ANTOINE goes to open)

ANTOINE. (off) My dear Giraffe! Incline your head towards my lips! (Kiss)

GEORGIE. (off) Hello Antoine.

ANTOINE. (off) And that is Basil, the Great!

(They enter)

May I call you by your first name straight away? Actually I won't call you Basil. I have this little habit of calling 'human beings' - so called - by animal names. She is my giraffe and Frank is my hedgehog. (Looks intently at BASIL)

BASIL. Hello Frank!

FRANK. Hello to you!

ANTOINE. And he is going to be my slick little pig! Slickety pig.

(FRANK laughs)

FRANK. Antoine, you mustn't offend him like that!

ANTOINE. Of course, I may. After all I am Antoine. (To BASIL and GEORGIE) Recline and rest your bodies in my oh-so-soft armchairs...and have some punch, my dears! Punch, the drink of the gods!

FRANK. Slickety pig! (Laughs)

GEORGIE. You should laugh with a name like hedgehog.

BASIL. I thought I was going to get hash to smoke. I can wait for the punch.

ANTOINE. You'll get all your heart's desires.

BASIL. And what animal are you?

ANTOINE. Me? I am the highest ranking power among the animals. (Reflects) I am the jellyfish. (Laughs. Passes a cigarette to BASIL) There you are slickety pig. Draw hard, inhale deep and leave it there. Let your lungs burst!

(BASIL inhales)

How are you, my little giraffe?

GEORGIE. Not too bad, thanks.

(ANTOINE passes her a cigarette and one to FRANK. ANTOINE smokes a pipe. Silence while they smoke)

BASIL. Smells like in a church.

ANTOINE. Right, slickety pig! It has a lot to do with God too. Inhale my friend! Inhale deep! You've got to inhale hash deep.

GEORGIE. (to BASIL) Do you notice anything?

BASIL. My head is beginning to fill.

ANTOINE. Have some punch, slickety pig! Punch, giraffe! Punch, hedgehog!

FRANK. Yes, please! (Pours) Basil, tell Antoine what happened at the reception.

ANTOINE. Yes, please do. Please tell us.

BASIL. How many more times?

ANTOINE. You haven't told me yet, please, slickety pig!

BASIL. Well, there isn't much to tell. I took my clothes off...

ANTOINE. Tell it slowly. This has to be savoured. Come on, slickety pig!

BASIL. First of all, I don't like my new nickname.

ANTOINE. All right, you can be a shark!

BASIL. And secondly I can't stand that dirge.

ANTOINE. That's Tchaikovsky!

BASIL. Tchaikovsky or no Tchaikovsky... (Giggles) Tchaikovsky or... or no Tchaikovsky...You can stuff this music up your arse. (Giggles)

ANTOINE. Slickety pig, you are offending a God!'

BASIL. God is dead...there is no God...

(Rises, the drugs are beginning to take effect)

the whole world is... (Giggling)

GEORGIE. Beginning to feel something?

BASIL. Some imagination...hell...Hell is other people...

FRANK. (casually in time to the music) Manipulation... (Whistles, winks at ANTOINE)

ANTOINE. Tell us, shark! (Moves to BASIL, grips his arm) Tell us, shark dear.

(GEORGIE starts to giggle)

(To GEORGIE) You high?

GEORGIE. My, my'. (Giggles)

FRANK. Tell us about the French...

BASIL. Well, I came in...and there are all the artists...
all those Michelangelos standing in a line like house-
wives queueing outside the breadshop.

ANTOINE. Those Michelangelos! How right you are!

BASIL. There I am and I ask them: anything being given
away free here? And what do you think they were
doing? They were all queueing to see the Minister
for the Arts...and what do you think they got?

ANTOINE. What?

BASIL. A warm handshake! I mean, a soggy handshake.
Because if I shake hands with three hundred people I'm
bound to get wet hands. So I thought, I'll get into line
as well...I had a look at their faces...each one looked
more idiotic than the next, and they were all grinning
at the Minister...they were all...ah, now the reefer's
beginning to work...

ANTOINE. Tell us more! (Watching BASIL intently)

BASIL. I get up to him...and I say: Bon soir, Monsieur.
The Minister, quick...quick on the uptake thinks I'm
French. He says: Bon soir, Monsieur. So I say:
Beg your pardon, but I am as British as Roastbeef
and Yorkshire Pudding. I was only pretending.

(ANTOINE and GEORGIE laugh)

ANTOINE. (to FRANK) The man's a genius. Go on!

BASIL. Well, and then, a bit later, came the Speech.
Richards gave me a sign and I started my strip act.
The Minister (Chuckles) got red in the face...he

was just talking about the message of art...and when I'd finished the police arrived. Hugh took some photos of me, I said 'Bon Soir' to the Minister and they took me away. They wouldn't let me get dressed until we got back to the office.

GEORGIE. Wouldn't let you! (Laughs) Did you want to get dressed?

BASIL. Well...I did feel a bit stupid.

ANTOINE. Extremely interesting. Extreeeemely interesting! Have some punch, shark! Drink! Have some of this! (Passes him a tablet)

(BASIL swallows it)

BASIL (kicks the record player. The needle slides) Turn off...that barrel organ!

(GEORGIE laughs)

That old crock! (Turns the Tchaikovsky record on to 45 revolutions) That old box... (Begins to laugh wildly)

GEORGIE. The old box...of Mr. Cox. (Laughter)

BASIL. Box, cox, fox, pox.

GEORGIE. Mr. Cox... (Laughter)

BASIL. (laughs. Kicks record cabinet) Record box! (Laughs)

ANTOINE. Shark. Control yourself. Shark!

BASIL. (kicking) I'm a shark...hark, hark, hark. (Plays at being a shark, bites GEORGIE) I'm the fastest shark... (Laughs)

(GEORGIE laughs)

ANTOINE. I'm the jelly fish. Hello! Jellyfish!

BASIL. The shark can bark!

(All laugh except FRANK)

ANTOINE. The jelly with a belly! Shark, eat the jelly with a belly...jelly-fishy-wish!

BASIL. Giraffe, don't laugh. (Laughs) Laugh, laugh, laugh!

(BASIL rushes round the room, knocking down objects, damaging furniture)

FRANK. Be careful! You're not at home!

BASIL. The hedgehog's in the bog! Lock, lock, lock!

ANTOINE. Jellyfish calling shark! Jellyfish calling shark! Jellyfish calling shark! Jelly into the melee!

BASIL. I'm the fast shark! Hark, hark!

GEORGIE. Shark! Hark!

ANTOINE. (approaches BASIL) Jelly to shark. Jelly to shark. (Kisses BASIL lightly on the cheek)

(BASIL pushes him away, kicks him)

BASIL. Shark to jellyfish! Shark to jellyfish!

(Throws ANTOINE onto sofa, pushes him with foot. ANTOINE giggles)

Shark to jellyfish! Shark to jellyfish!

(ANTOINE screams and giggles)

GEORGIE. (to FRANK) My dear hedgehog...why are you sitting alone in your bog?

FRANK. (deliberate) Ha-ha.

(BASIL stands up straight shaking with laughter. ANTOINE and GEORGIE are gasping for breath.

GEORGIE rises, puts her hand over BASIL's
mouth, then gives him a long kiss)

ANTOINE. Shark swallows giraffe! Shark swallows giraffe!

Jellyfish swallows shark. (Rushes at BASIL) Rrrrr!

GEORGIE. The shark can bark!

(All laugh except FRANK. Pause)

BASIL. Well, giraffe, when are you going to sleep with the
shark? (Glances at FRANK)

FRANK. You're all bloody idiots!

(They breathe heavily, then sit and rest)

Smoke a bit of hash and there they are all flat out on
the floor. Well, I must say, you're a lot...

BASIL. (after a pause) Georgie girl, I'm going to kill myself.

(He and GEORGIE laugh wildly and look at FRANK)

FRANK. (to GEORGIE) Okay...

GEORGIE. Okay.

ANTOINE. (taking a book from a shelf) Now then. The
shark is going to read to us.

FRANK. What is it?

ANTOINE Fairy tales...for children with strong nerves.
Come on, read us a bit, dearest shark.

BASIL. Let the hedgehog read. He is the clever one...the
sober one. (Laughs)

ANTOINE. Come on, Frankie-hog.

(They laugh)

Or are you afraid?

FRANK. What are you talking about? Why should I read you fairy tales?

ANTOINE. Oh, come on.

FRANK. Whatever for?

ANTOINE. Because we are all dear little children and we're going to listen attentively...

BASIL. Read to us, uncle hedgehog!

FRANK. (laughs) My God, you're all idiots!

GEORGIE. Please, uncle hedgehog, read to us!

FRANK. (opens the book smiling) What sort of fairy tales are these?

ANTOINE. The best from the world over.

FRANK. All right, just to keep the kids quiet. Which one do you want me to read?

ANTOINE. Where the bookmark is.

FRANK. The tale of the little tree. Right?

ANTOINE. Quite right, hedgehog my dearest. Anyone want some more punch?

(They shake their heads)

FRANK. All right. The Tale of The Little Tree.

(FRANK tries to sound gay. GEORGIE rests her head against BASIL's shoulder)

Once upon a time there were a man and his wife. Once upon a time...oh...(Reads on) They had a nice, big house and a nice, big garden. In the garden there were many flowers, planted in pretty, well-kept beds.

Indeed it was hard work to keep it all in good order...
hhmm, Everyone who passed the garden remarked,
what a wonderful garden. But the greatest pride of
the couple and of the garden was a little tree.

(FRANK smiles at the others who never take their
eyes off him)

...was a little tree. But the little tree gave them much
trouble. It did not seem to want to grow. It stood
right in the centre of the garden but it did not want to
grow into a proper tree. (FRANK stops)

ANTOINE   Carry on, hedgehog!

FRANK.. ...did not want to grow into a proper tree. The
little tree had been planted many years ago, but it
just would not grow. Nor did it want to strand up...
eh... stand up straight.

(There is laughter as he misreads the word)

the two old people had to protect and sup-prect...eh
...support the tree against wind and weather. At the
slightest breath of wind the little tee...eh tree...
would fall over...Someone else read this.

ANTOINE. Read on, hedgehog, read on.

BASIL. Read on, uncle!

FRANK. (hurrying on) Often the wife said: how poorly our
little tree looks, how it shivers and shrinks. I hope
it will survive the winter. Many times the man lifted
it out of the earth and planted it somewhere else,
adding fertile soil, but soon afterwards it would fall
over. The little lee...eh...the little tree was plitty...
pretty but not strong enough. It just did not have
sufficient stength...strength... (FRANK tosses the
book onto the floor) This is dull.

ANTOINE. But it's terribly exciting!

GEORGIE. You aren't the world's greatest reader!

(BASIL presses his face against GEORGIE's dress
and laughs)

FRANK. (to GEORGIE, rising) Are you coming?

GEORGIE. What?

FRANK. I'm going.

GEORGIE. Well, go then.

FRANK. Come with me.

GEORGIE. Why should I?

FRANK. Because I'm not feeling well.

(BASIL laughs, GEORGIE giggles)

ANTOINE. Have some punch.

FRANK. Come on now, please.

GEORGIE. Are you depressed or something?

FRANK. (goes out) I'll wait for you outside.

(GEORGIE rises and follows him out)

GEORGIE. Good-bye, my loves.

ANTOINE. Farewell, giraffe! (Accompanies her out and
returns. To BASIL) Have some punch, shark. Ah
well, some people can take it, others can't. (Looks
at BASIL) You can take it all right. Let me hug you,
my precious. Have some punch, shark.

BASIL. Okay, but I need filling up.

(ANTOINE pours him some)

ANTOINE. (passing him his pipe) Have a puff, slickety pig.

(BASIL draws, rises. ANTOINE looks through BASIL's
folder)

61

Great...absolutely great. (Comes closer to BASIL, grips his arm) Come with me.

BASIL. Where?

ANTOINE. (vaguely) Over there.

BASIL. What for?

ANTOINE. Hop into beddie-byes.

BASIL. I'm going.

ANTOINE. Stay here, shark.

BASIL. Why?

ANTOINE. Live with me.

BASIL. What for?

ANTOINE. (kissing him on the ear) Don't be silly! Have some more punch. (Pause)

BASIL. Are you going to buy this picture?

ANTOINE. Of course I am.

BASIL. How much will you give me for it?

ANTOINE. £100.

BASIL. 500.

ANTOINE. All right...500, but only because it's you.

BASIL. Give me the money then.

ANTOINE. (goes to get the money) All right, if you don't trust me. Oh well, sharks are distrustful. (Hands BASIL £500)

(BASIL takes the money)

BASIL. Cheerio, jellyfish. (Starts to go)

ANTOINE. (clinging to him) Stay here, you silly boy.

BASIL. There is the picture. (Pushes him away)

ANTOINE. (returns) Don't be stupid, slickety pig. Don't
be so stupid. You don't know what I can do for you.
Just think!

(BASIL picks up a glass, breaks off the stem and
approaches ANTOINE. ANTOINE withdraws, BASIL
follows, ANTOINE stops, BASIL comes close to him
and presses the glass against ANTOINE's forehead.
ANTOINE screams)

CURTAIN

SCENE SIX

(The Kitchen. LADY DE MARLIMONT, smartly
dressed, GEORGIE and BASIL are sitting at the table,
eating and drinking)

BASIL. (in a good mood) One hundred - he says. For a
hundred you won't even get my autograph, I said to
him. Anyway, I said, I won't give you my autograph,
because the fetishists live in the Congo or on the
Amazon in Brazil and that is where he should get himself dropped by the next helicopter.

(All laugh)

And what do you think he does, the bloody fool? He
gets out his wallet and offers me five hundred! Ha!
Then I see that he's got at least another two hundred
in his wallet...well, wallet, more of a notecase...
so I say to him, you can throw those in as well and
then we can talk about art! Hehehehe! that's how he
laughed.

LADY DE M. You'd better be careful that the tax people
don't take it all away.

BASIL. If they do, even if they take fifty percent, I'll still
have three hundred and fifty for that picture - and it
wasn't particularly good either. That's not too bad,
eh?

GEORGIE. Which picture was it?

BASIL. It's called: "Where is the artist"...a long row of
hedges. He can spend hours every day trying to spot
me and his guests can have a go at trying to spot me,
and everybody who goes there can try to spot me.
Look a little closer...(Eating)...look there...can you
spot him? There! There he is the scoundrel who got
£700 out of me. (Laughs) And best of all, Hugh
Richards, Professor of History of Art and Art Critic
of a leading daily stands there saying: Oh well, seven
hundred isn't too much for all those leaves and twigs
and sticks and a head full of straw. Hahaha, did he
laugh.

LADY DE M. You're a one! I said to myself straight away,
the first time I saw him (Pointing at BASIL) He's
going to go a long way. I didn't know in what direction,
but I knew he'd go a long way. I could have sworn it...
I could have sworn it...(She rises, pours champagne,
sings: Tralalala)

GEORGIE. Food all right?

BASIL. (fascinated by the voluptuous forms of LADY DE
MARLIMONT's body) You're looking exceptionally
well today, darling.

GEORGIE. Go on...

BASIL. Not you...I mean your Mum.

LADY DE M. (happily) Thank you, kind sir!

GEORGIE. Want some more to drink?

LADY DE M. We've run dry. That was the last drop my darlings.

BASIL. Oh. Well, somebody go and get some. Georgie? Are you going to get some?

GEORGIE. What, me?

LADY DE M. Well, do you expect him to go? It's his big day today.

GEORGIE. I feel sick.

BASIL. Why do you feel sick?

GEORGIE. Don't ask stupid questions.

BASIL. But why?

GEORGIE. Because of the baby, nitwit!

BASIL. Does that make you feel sick?

LADY DE M. He's a sweetie!

BASIL. No one feels sick because of my little fellow. That's a personal insult to me! Off you go.

LADY DE M. Why don't you, the fresh air will do you good.

BASIL. Go on, Georgie, pussy, go and get us something.

GEORGIE. Let's both go.

BASIL. You're not a little girlie anymore.

LADY DE M. Off you pop.

BASIL. (gives money to GEORGIE) There you are, get us three bottles of the same.

GEORGIE. (taking money) You devil!

BASIL. My God, I don't know, women are so complicated,

not only women, everybody. Everybody is so complicated, what do you think, Mummy?

LADY DE M. I can't understand any of them. I don't know, we used to have such fun. We always found time to do things and work at the same time. I was on the stage... I couldn't afford to stay in bed all day. I would have got bored with it anyway. You're a layabout too, I suppose, but at least you've got some talent, you can afford to lounge about and, looking at it from the practical angle, you're rolling in money, at least for the time being. And that's all that matters, let's be honest. Whoever comes to me, whoever he is, if he hasn't got the lolly, he can lump it. No money, no music!

BASIL. You're so right, Mummy. Frank isn't right for Georgie.

LADY DE M. I think you've already managed to convince her of that.

BASIL. But I'm not right for her either.

LADY DE M. Don't say that, she is just like me, she needs a crook like you. Anyway she's fallen for you head over heels.

BASIL. That doesn't mean anything. Do you know, Mum, what I need?

LADY DE M. I don't think you need a woman at all...

BASIL. Oh yes, I do. I need someone like you.

LADY DE M. For your collection, maybe, but not really.

BASIL. You may be right. But I know I need you terribly just now, Mum.

LADY DE M. (ruffles his hair) I am 43 years old, old enough to be your mother.

BASIL. So what? That's no age.

66

LADY DE M. You're right, you know. I don't know why people go by figures like 43.

BASIL. It's all shit. I want you and you want me. What are we waiting for? Eh? (Goes to Hall door) What kind of state is he in?

LADY DE M. He's asleep, he's had an injection.

BASIL. (putting on a record) An injection... (He massages her shoulders, working on them for some time)

LADY DE M. You're a monster, Basil.

(He spreads the rug on the floor with his feet)

BASIL. Come along, Madam.

LADY DE M. You're nuts. In any case Georgie will be back any minute.

BASIL. By the time she gets back we'll be finished, eh? We'll be through by then, the two of us, Mummy.

LADY DE M. Let's do it tomorrow or somewhere else.

BASIL. Here and now! Now and here!

(He pulls her down, she tries to push him away, he hits out at her, pulls off her top)

Don't make such a fuss.

LADY DE M. Stop it!

BASIL. (throws himself on top of her) Here and now! (Raising his voice) Here and now!

(GEORGIE enters, BASIL carries on)

GEORGIE. Oh, charming! Very nice! Very nice indeed. Just you wait!

(She runs off. BASIL struggles with LADY DE MARLI-MONT)

LADY DE M. Stop it, she's going to do something to herself.

BASIL. She won't come to any harm.

(GEORGIE's voice is heard)

GEORGIE. (off) Daddy, come and look. Have a look at what she's up to...look.

(She enters, leading her sick father by the hand and pulling him through the door)

GEORGIE. Just look at that.

(The old man begins to gasp for breath. LADY DE MARLIMONT screams, the old man collapses)

LADY DE M. Call the doctor!

GEORGIE. Not me!

(LADY DE MARLIMONT slaps her face)

LADY DE M. God, I could...

CURTAIN

SCENE SEVEN

(The Kitchen. GEORGIE, visibly pregnant, is cooking. A saucepan is steaming. Pop music from Radio One. FRANK enters)

FRANK. Hallo there.

GEORGIE. Hallo. All over?

FRANK. I think so. Mind you, I didn't go into the church. I think it's ridiculous that they should have a church wedding.

GEORGIE. Well, Mummy wanted it.

FRANK. Basil didn't.

GEORGIE. Basil said, he likes a church wedding because he likes the smell of hash in the church.

FRANK. Bloody idiot. And you're cooking for them?

GEORGIE. Any objections?

FRANK. I really don't understand you.

GEORGIE. Why not?

FRANK. Well.

GEORGIE. Why not!

FRANK. First he gets you pregnant, then he marries your mother - and there you are cooking away for them. What are you making?

GEORGIE. Spaghetti.

FRANK. You don't say. As a first course.

GEORGIE. No, main course.

FRANK. Is the wedding lunch somewhere else then?

GEORGIE. No, here.

FRANK. And you're making spaghetti?

GEORGIE. It's Basil's favourite dish. He eats it three times a week.

FRANK. Don't be ridiculous.

GEORGIE. Did Antoine come?

FRANK. Oh yes, lots of people came. And Hugh took photographs like mad...acted like a Hollywood

director he did. Then they took a picture of Mummy
holding Basil in her arms like a baby...and one where
Basil stands with his foot on her and she is lying on
the ground, and Antoine went leaping around like a goat
and kept calling your mother 'llama'.

GEORGIE. Try some of this.

FRANK. (tasting) It's hot...not bad.

GEORGIE. Could you lay the table?

FRANK. What me?

(GEORGIE kisses him)

GEORGIE. You're not cross, are you?

FRANK. Oh, all right. (Starts to lay the table) This place
is a madhouse.

GEORGIE. Look, it's quite simple. I'll have the baby and then
we can get married.

FRANK. Ha! You don't think I'm going to work my fingers
to the bone to keep that brat of Basil's, do you? You're..

GEORGIE. No, Mummy is going to keep the baby.

FRANK. (laying the table) How many will there be?

GEORGIE. Basil, Mummy, Hugh, Antoine, you and myself -
that's six.

FRANK. What a collection. It's not easy to sort out the
various relationships.

GEORGIE. You're slowly turning into a good old square.

FRANK. No chance. Where are the happy couple going to
sit?

GEORGIE. Wherever you like.

(ANTOINE's voice is heard outside:)

Heave ho!

BASIL. (enters, carrying LADY DE MARLIMONT) You're not at all heavy!

(He puts her down. LADY DE MARLIMONT tries to kiss BASIL. He is about to turn away, she pulls him back and grabs him wildly)

ANTOINE. What a delicious smell! Is that my super, special sauce? (Looks into saucepan, tastes) Outch! It's hot!

LADY DE M. My goodness, children, I am glad all this fuss and bother is over and done with. Food ready, Georgie?

GEORGIE. Yes.

ANTOINE. Our giraffe is an excellent cook. Only it's a bit too hot! (Giggles, looks at FRANK)

BASIL. Hi, Frank, how are you, you old hog! Why didn't you come to church? Believe me, it was tremendous. I'm telling you. It was a dream wedding!

FRANK. Good.

ANTOINE. You know why he didn't go in, don't you: because the wicked can't stand churches.

(Everyone smiles)

FRANK. Naturally, Antoine, I suppose that's why you were there.

(Smiles painfully)

ANTOINE. Ah well, I'm a saint anyway.

LADY DE M. You've laid the table - that's nice of you Georgie love.

GEORGIE. I didn't lay the table. Frank did it.

LADY DE M. Frankie, my love, how nice of you.

BASIL. Frankie, the pride of the family! We'll let him eat with us, shall we? What do you say, Frankie.

FRANK. Okay, okay, Basil, we know you're super.

BASIL. Lost your powers of speech boyo? Tell us, you're not sulking again, are you. People who sulk will not be allowed in here today. Either you laugh or you go! Laugh! Dear friend!

FRANK. (artificial laugh) Ha-ha-ha.

BASIL. Well, I must say, that was very convincing. (To GEORGIE, embracing her) And how is my little giraffe?

GEORGIE. Very well, thanks.

BASIL. (caressing her) And what is that little scoundrel doing inside there?

GEORGIE. Nothing.

BASIL. Nothing, that's not much.

GEORGIE. Well, you don't expect him to ride around on a bike like you, do you?

BASIL. Why not? What do you think, Mum?

LADY DE M. God, I am looking forward to seeing this little fellow. Just as if he were my own. Well, I suppose he is in a way.

BASIL. (sits at the table and rattles his knife and fork) Sit down, Mama!

LADY DE M. I must go and change.

BASIL. No, you mustn't go and change. Sit down!

LADY DE M. In a minute.

BASIL. Sit down, I said!

(LADY DE MARLIMONT sits)

GEORGIE. Could you give me a hand, Frank.

FRANK. What with?

GEORGIE. Hold that dish!

(FRANK holds the dish)

BASIL. Hurry up, chef. Hahahaha.

FRANK. All in good time.

GEORGIE. Hold it steady, don't wobble.

ANTOINE. He's a wobbler, my little hedgehog is.

FRANK. All right, jellyfish.

BASIL. Throw us some spaghetti, Frank!

(FRANK takes the dish to the table)

GEORGIE. Where is Hugh? (Doorbell) Ah, talk of the
    devil. Would you go and open the door, Frank...

(FRANK goes. BASIL begins to eat greedily)

All right?

BASIL. No need to ask.

(LADY DE MARLIMONT begins to cry)

ANTOINE. Why are you crying, llama?

LADY DE M. It's nothing.

BASIL. My wife is moved. Am I right, Mummy?

LADY DE M. It's all right. I'm better now. It was just the strain.

RICHARDS. God be with you!

BASIL. Welcome, great critic!

RICHARDS. You eating already?

BASIL. Come and join us or it'll all be gone.

RICHARDS. Hang on. Just before I do, I'd like to take a few more photos. En famille, you might say. The maestro eating spaghetti, not bad eh? (Looks through camera) Just like that, Basil. Great. Now with your wife. Splendid.

BASIL. Come here, Georgie pussy.

RICHARDS. Smile! Okay.

ANTOINE. (begging like a dog) Jellyfish would like to be photographed too.

RICHARDS. All right. You join them over there. That's it. Frank, could you move over a bit, or your hand will be in the picture.

FRANK. Are you going to make a movie about the O'Malley family? Rather like the Trapp family...

RICHARDS. Talking of the Trapp family - Madam, you used to be a singer?

LADY DE M. I was.

RICHARDS. Shouldn't we take one then, where you are singing?

LADY DE M. But why?

ANTOINE. Sing, llama, trill.

BASIL. Of course she can sing, she sings like a blackbird,

my little birdie.

LADY DE M. Get away with you. That's all in the past!

BASIL. Listen, my love, you're going to sing now, see, because your Basil likes it, he would like to see your bell-like voice in the photograph.

LADY DE M. Well, I'll pretend I'm singing and you take the picture.

BASIL. You'll sing, or else...

ANTOINE. The shark commands, the llama sings. That's nature's law - red in tooth and claw.

RICHARDS. Ready.

LADY DE M. (sings) 'We'll gather lilacs in the spring again...'

ANTOINE. Enchanting.

BASIL. That's made me really hungry, the way you open your mouth so wide. Let's eat.

(They eat)

LADY DE M. If only my dear Charles could have seen this.

BASIL. He'd drop dead again.

(Laughter. They eat)

RICHARDS. I don't usually like spaghetti, but the way Georgie cooks it, it's super.

ANTOINE. Superbly delicious...superbly delicious.

(They eat)

BASIL. (after a pause) Frank, would you get me the pepper?

FRANK. How do I know where the pepper is?

GEORGIE. Up on the shelf on the left.

FRANK. (rises) What do you mean up on the shelf on the left?

GEORGIE. There!

FRANK. I'd call that in the middle to the right.

(They eat in silence for some time)

ANTOINE. (maliciously) Hedgehog...would you get me some salt.

(All begin to laugh. They laugh more and more)

FRANK. You must be joking.

LADY DE M. Frankie, would you get me a glass of water?

FRANK. Shut up, stupid cow! You superannuated tart!

LADY DE M. How dare you?

BASIL. Speak like that to my wife!

FRANK. You shut up, you puppet you, you manipulated puppet.

(Tosses spaghetti at BASIL and LADY DE MARLIMONT)

RICHARDS. Don't do that, Frankie.

LADY DE M. Get out of my house, at once! Get out! Basil, throw him out!

BASIL. Get lost, Frankie! If you soil my beautiful body, you are no longer my friend!

FRANK. Why should I go? I'm beginning to enjoy myself. It's beginning to look a bit more colourful. I'll go when I feel like it! I'm not afraid of you waxworks. You can kiss my arse, you and your dream wedding!

(He knocks over the table. BASIL starts to fight
FRANK. They fight with their fists, but the fight ends
undecided)

LADY DE M. I'm going to call the police. (Exit)

GEORGIE. Frankie, you're out of your mind!

ANTOINE. The hedgehog is fuming!

RICHARDS. Shame about the spaghetti.

(Fight ends)

FRANK. Bastards! (To ANTOINE and RICHARDS) You're
great, you are. First you talk big, then you don't have
the guts to go through with it. There they are sucking
up to him, clinging to him like...like limpets.

LADY DE M. (enters) The Police are on their way.

RICHARDS. You don't say. We're going to have some fun.
I must put in a new film. (Puts new film into camera)

BASIL. Ladies and gentlemen, make yourselves at home.
Pretend nothing has happened. Georgie, puss, get
some wine. Nothing has happened...because when
Frank tries to get something done, nothing ever
happens.

ANTOINE. Well, if I might be allowed to comment on all
this...I think it's all remarkable...quite remarkable.

BASIL. (pours wine) There you are...take a glass each...
cheers!

ANTOINE. Cheers!

RICHARDS. Cheers, maestro!

(FRANK lights a cigarette. They drink. Doorbell.
GEORGIE puts on a record)

LADY DE M. (goes to the door) I'm glad you've come. He's

in there, the one with the cigarette.

(The POLICEMEN stop a short distance away from
FRANK)

Look, Officer, what a mess he has made, that lunatic...

1st POLICE OFFICER. Let's go, young man.

2nd POLICE OFFICER. What are you waiting for, an
invitation?

FRANK. (snatches a kitchen knife) Come here, you bastards,
if you dare....

1st OFFICER. Let's go.

FRANK. Just you try, Fascist Pig!

(FRANK makes as if to attack the 1st POLICE OFFICER
with his knife. The 2nd OFFICER grabs him from behind. FRANK swings round, is thrown off his balance
by POLICEMAN's foot and falls hitting his head on edge
of table. LADY DE MARLIMONT and GEORGIE scream)

BASIL. A hit, a hit, a palpable hit!

(RICHARDS takes photographs)

CURTAIN

SCENE EIGHT

(Hospital Ward. There are about five beds with
patients. Night. There is a strong wind outside.
One of the patients groans at regular intervals.
FRANK tosses and turns in a bed in the foreground.
He sits up, turns on his bedside lamp, takes a packet
of cigarettes and lights one)

1st PATIENT. (sleepy) There he goes stinking the place
out again... (Turns over)

2nd PATIENT. Do you have to pollute the air? (Pause)
　　You might at least open the window.

FRANK. Okay.

　　(FRANK gets out of bed, opens a window, the wind
　　blows in. FRANK sits on his bed. MR. MIDDLETON
　　wakes up)

MIDDLETON. (next to FRANK) What's happening?

2nd PATIENT. The artist is stinking the place out again.

1st PATIENT. I don't care what he does as long as he closes
　　the window.

2nd PATIENT. What time is it?

1st PATIENT. (looking at the clock by his bed) I make it
　　three.

MIDDLETON. I only make it half past two.

1st PATIENT. Your clock is always slow.

MIDDLETON. On the contrary, it usually keeps very good
　　time. I only had it repaired the other day.

1st PATIENT. It's ten to three! The middle of the night.

MIDDLETON. I make it twenty to three. What time do you
　　make it, Mr. Edgar?

2nd PATIENT. I make it exactly half past.

MIDDLETON. Half past what?

2nd PATIENT. Half past twelve. No, that can't be right.
　　It must have stopped.

MIDDLETON. What time do you make it, Mr. Swann?

FRANK. I haven't got a watch.

MIDDLETON. There's a clock above the door, can you see it?

1st PATIENT. It says a quarter to three.

2nd PATIENT. Two minutes to.

MIDDLETON. I expect that one is correct.

1st PATIENT. It's only a cheap clock.

MIDDLETON. Cheap clocks often work perfectly.

1st PATIENT. Would you please close that window? We'll all catch our death. It's snowing outside.

2nd PATIENT. The window will remain open as long as he is smoking. You're not going to die because of a bit of fresh air.

1st PATIENT. If you like I'll ring for Nurse and ask her to take you for a walk outside!

2nd PATIENT. Excellent idea. (He rings for a nurse)

MIDDLETON. Gentlemen, we're not going to quarrel, are we. After all, we're all in the same boat.

1st PATIENT. People in such good health as yourself aren't supposed to be in hospital at all!

MIDDLETON. I think we'll leave the verdict to the consultant and house physician.

(NURSE PEGGY enters)

PEGGY. You've all got your lights on? Is there anything wrong, duckies? And the window is open! Are you out of your minds!

1st PATIENT. I'm going to complain to the House Physician tomorrow.

PEGGY. (closes the window) But Grandpa! (Kisses his

80

cheek and slaps it playfully) There you are, it's already closed, Daddy, and now you're all going to be good boys and go to sleep. And our Frankie here is going to put out his cigarette and turn off the light. (FRANK puts out cigarette) Or else, the boss is going to be cross.

MIDDLETON. Nurse Peggy?

PEGGY. What is it Mr. Middleton?

MIDDLETON. Would you get me a cup of hot cocoa?

PEGGY. What, now?

MIDDLETON. (offering her a chocolate) Here you are. It's got a rum filling. If you bring me that cocoa, I'll give you another one.

PEGGY. Very well. But you must keep quiet until all our grumpies have fallen asleep. (Exit)

MIDDLETON. (to FRANK - the others rest and groan) Peggy is an angel. Without her I wouldn't be here any more.

FRANK. Why not?

MIDDLETON. I've been a picture of health for the last month. But dear little Peggy puts the curve up on my temperature chart every time I'm due to be discharged.

FRANK. What do you mean?

MIDDLETON. I want to stay! You're a young man, you'll probably think, he's talking nonsense, the old fool! But what am I going to do at home? Specially now during the winter. I've got to heat the place, I've got to cook for myself, I can't afford a housekeeper. I can go to my nephew's to watch the telly but that's a long way from my place and they don't want me there all the time either. So what shall I do? I've got my food here, there are people I can talk to, or at least have a row with, I can watch the telly, go for a walk...

what more do you want? The only unpleasant time
of the day is the doctor's visit, and having to pretend
to be a sick man all the time. But then I've got to
save my face in front of the other patients.

FRANK. All on the National Health!

MIDDLETON. That's what it's there for, isn't it? I've
never been sick, maybe three or four times in all my
life. But I've never been in hospital before. The
funniest thing is, the last time I was due to be discharged I took my temperature and guess what? I
really did have a temperature, nearly 100. A real
temperature. I suppose it's psychosomatic.

PEGGY. (enters with cocoa) Now, drink up quickly and
turn off your light! (She turns off both lamps) Nightie-
night!

MIDDLETON. Your chocolate!

PEGGY. I'll have it tomorrow, shshsh.

MIDDLETON. Good night, Mr. Swann.

FRANK. Good night.

(Pause)

MIDDLETON. Excellent cocoa. (Pause) The food is better
than in many restaurants. Ah。

(He settles down. The wind howls outside, patients
groan, one of them dreams aloud)

The major is dreaming about the lion again. Every
night he attacks him!

VOICE. Bloody Lion! Get away! Get away!

MIDDLETON. It's more amusing than going to the theatre.
(Pause) It's just like going to the theatre...after all,
normally I never go to the theatre.

(Pause. Some groans. In the distnce, inside the
hospital, the sound of laughter and of a transistor
playing. BASIL and GEORGIE, the latter very drunk,
enter)

BASIL. In here! This is the ward of wards!

GEORGIE. But it's all dark!

BASIL. Let there be light!

(FRANK turns on his light, so does MIDDLETON)

FRANK. Are you mad? Don't make so much noise!

BASIL. But Frankie, my boy! Day is night and night is day.
(Shouts) Wakey, wakey! Good morning! Rise and
shine!

(GEORGIE laughs hysterically)

Time for your daily dozen!

FRANK. Shut up!

BASIL. I thought you would be pleased if we came to see you!

FRANK. How on earth did you get in?

GEORGIE. (teasing him) How on earth did you get in...
Frankie pussy... Frankie love... are you poorly, luvey?
Puss is cross... (Gets into bed with FRANK)

FRANK. Go on, get out!

GEORGIE. Get out, he says. But Frankie my love...
(Kisses him) Frankie pussy...

MIDDLETON. She's a bit of a passionate one! (With pleasure)
A creature of true breeding!

(The other PATIENTS wake up and watch from their
beds with horror and surprise)

1st PATIENT. That's the limit!

2nd PATIENT. Nurse!

BASIL. Gentlemen! Calm yourselves! Have a good look
at those two lovebirds! Have a good look - see,
gentlemen! Out you get! (Shakes the bed of the man
who groans) Out you get, mate! (Turns up volume
of transistor radio. The sick man groans) Look,
how she's gobbling him up, the little whore.

FRANK. Cut it out! Don't be an idiot.

(She clutches him tightly, he pushes her away. NURSE
PEGGY enters)

PEGGY. Who are you?

BASIL. Who am I? Who are you? Little mouse.

PEGGY. What are you doing here?

2nd PATIENT. Get that comedian out of here. (Rising) I'm
going to get the house officer.

PEGGY. You're that painter, aren't you, that crazy one...
Basil O' Malley!

BASIL. Right first time! She knows me, the little mouse.

(Hugs her)

PEGGY. Let go!

BASIL. Let go, little mo! (Laughs, lets go of her, gives
her a push, she runs out) See you!

(Turns volume up)

1st PATIENT. This is too much!

MIDDLETON. (to FRANK) I don't mind in the least...for
someone like myself, in good health, it makes a pleasant
change!

BASIL. (to MIDDLETON) Come and swing a leg with me, great-grandad! (Pulls him out of bed and makes as if to dance with him)

FRANK. Get out!

(Slaps GEORGIE's face)

MIDDLETON. My dear sir, I'm afraid I don't know how to dance. I'm sure your lady-wife here can dance much better!

GEORGIE. Frankie is cross!

(Dances wildly with BASIL. They dance away from each other, back to back, making ecstatic movements. BASIL stumbles, pulls down the bedclothes, jumps onto FRANK's bed and dances)

FRANK. (leaps up) Get off, scram! (Pushes him off the bed) Who do you think you are! Bloody fool!

BASIL. Well said, Frankie. (Egging him on)

FRANK. Bloody country bumpkin, upstart! You primitive ape!

(BASIL encourages him)

BASIL. Super. Carry on!

FRANK. Infiltrating parasite! Arse-crawling coward! (Hits out at him, BASIL laughs and dances away from him)

GEORGIE. Frankie is cross!

BASIL. Frankie is great! He's gigantic!

GEORGIE. He doesn't look gigantic though. He looks...He looks as if he's not at all well. Don't you think? (Dances)

2nd PATIENT. (outside) Doctor! Doctor! Help!

(Two other PATIENTS, in nightshirts, appear shyly at the door)

GEORGIE. Come and dance with us, Frankie!

1st PATIENT. (opens the window. The wind blows in some snow) Police!

GEORGIE. Frankie sweetie, don't you want to build him up? Don't you want to manipulate?

BASIL. Build me up, Frankie! Please, please, do build me up! I'm going to kill myself, Frankie...hahaha... look... (He winds a sheet round his neck, and falls to the ground laughing)

GEORGIE. (to FRANK) Why are you pulling such a sour face? Don't you have an urge to build something up? (Points to her stomach) Look, there's something for you to build up (Giggles) there's something to build up... something quite...fresh!

(FRANK hits her so that she falls to the ground, he goes on hitting at her, hitting her stomach, she screams)

BASIL. That's right, Frankie! Let her have it! You're great, Frankie!

(Gales howling through the window, snow, the PATIENTS calling, running about, utter chaos. DOCTOR and NURSES enter)

DOCTOR. What's going on? (To the NURSES) Help her up.

(They help GEORGIE up)

GEORGIE. (cries out with pain) Ouououou.

(GEORGIE is led outside)

DOCTOR. Who the hell are you? What are you doing in here?

BASIL. I shall feel insulted if you don't recognise me, sir!

DOCTOR. You must be out of your mind if you think you can behave like a hooligan in this hospital.

BASIL. My name is Basil O'Malley, if that means anything to you.

DOCTOR. O'Malley. I don't care what your name is. See that you leave here at once. (To PATIENTS) Quick march back into your beds. What do you think you are in here for? You too, Mr. Middleton. Or else you'll run a temperature again!

MIDDLETON. I feel a bit feverish already.

DOCTOR. And you too, Mr. Swann. I haven't experienced anything like this in my thirty years as a doctor!

2nd PATIENT. You see, doctor, it was like this...

DOCTOR. Go to sleep, I don't want to hear another word.

(A NURSE enters hurriedly)

NURSE. Geoffrey!

DOCTOR. What is it?

NURSE. She has lost the baby.

(The DOCTOR rushes out)

BASIL. (to FRANK) Cheerio then, I'm off home. You coming?

FRANK. What for?

BASIL. I expect Hugh will be there, and my wife... Antoine ... I don't suppose we shall get to bed before eight in the morning.

FRANK. I might come round later... when things have calmed down a bit.

BASIL. Yes, do come, dear old pal. Everything's back to

normal now. Like the good old days.

FRANK. Well...I suppose so. (Lights a cigarette)

BASIL. See you. (Exit)

1st PATIENT. Now he's smoking again.

SCENE NINE

(BASIL's Studio. Comfortably and expensively furnished, spacious. BASIL's WIFE asleep in an armchair. Next to her is a bottle of whisky, half empty. She snores loudly. Half a minute later BASIL enters. PEGGY, the Nurse, follows hesitantly)

BASIL. (to PEGGY) Asleep! (He creeps up to her, holds her nose, she lets out a distorted howl) The old sow's fighting for oxygen.

LADY DE M. Stop it, Basil.

BASIL. I'm extremely put out to find you...to find you in this state.

LADY DE M. Well, if you don't come home.

BASIL. (to PEGGY) Sit down, beautiful! (Offers her a chair)

LADY DE M. What have you got with you this time, who's this teenager?

BASIL. This isn't a teenager, duckie, this is a lady! A working woman! She works day and night!

LADY DE M. I can well imagine!

BASIL. Not the way you think, in your filthy bourgeois mind. She is a respectable lady. And she is going to stay the night with us. Eh, Peggy? And I shall make myself personally responsible to make sure that nothing indecent happens to her. That's why, in these exceptional circumstances she is going to sleep in my bed!

LADY DE M. Don't talk rubbish. You're mad! For three weeks now we've had these respectable ladies...

BASIL. Shut up! (Grips her, stares at her) Will you shut your trap. You know what happens, Mum, if you don't shut up. (Walks round the studio) Nothing but idle gossip.

LADY DE M. I'm leaving.

BASIL. That's just what you're waiting for, isn't it, you old sow. But you're going to stay here, because Richards will be here soon and he's quite keen on you, ducks. We'll all change round. Okay?

LADY DE M. That's what you think! Once and never again. You can keep your learned critic.

BASIL. Mummy, my love, don't you dare, I'm telling you. Richards is a friend of mine, don't you dare despise my friends.

PEGGY. I think I'd better go.

LADY DE M. Yes, you'd better.

BASIL. You're going to stay, beautiful! No-one's going. No-one's leaving, everyone's going to stay. We're going to get on very well together! You two are going to be the best of friends. Show Peggy the bed, love, and then she can go to bed whenever she's tired.

PEGGY. I'm not a bit tired.

BASIL. That's fine then. But you will be, very tired, believe me. (Looks around) What a mess. You, at forty-four, ought to have some sense of order! Why do you think I married you! An artist needs someone to keep things tidy for him. So: tidy up! Tidy up! That's your job! Show your good family background!

89

Ha! Old and messy too! What do you think of that, Peggy my gorgeous?

(Kisses PEGGY. LADY DE MARLIMONT begins to cry)

PEGGY. Look, she's crying.

BASIL. Crying? Out of the question, chick! (Moves to her) Come on, no crying now, understand? (Sings) 'Keep smiling through...' (She cries louder) Basil is with you and he loves you very much. 'Keep smiling through...'

LADY DE M. (to PEGGY) If you only knew what he gets up to every night. And I'm supposed to be...(cries)... I'm supposed to be his servant. And I do it for him, silly ass that I am!

PEGGY. But why are you doing it?

LADY DE M. You don't know what it's like when you love someone, and I do love that rascal! I love him so much, even though he's always hitting me. Why are you so cruel to me all the time. I do everything you ask of me.

BASIL. That'll do now. Go and wash your face. Richards will be here any minute and he doesn't like those watery crocodile eyes! He wants to see those two bright blue little sparklers in your face. Go and wash, put on some makeup and then tidy up a bit. Then we'll all love you. Okay? Say yes, honeybunch, say yes.

LADY DE M. Yes.

BASIL. You're a darling sweetiepie. (She goes out. To PEGGY) You look quite worn out, beautiful. You mustn't let the moods of my beloved spouse get you down!

PEGGY. Have you got a record player?

BASIL. Silly question. There it is. Wait a minute.

90

PEGGY. Got a Beatles record?

BASIL. Not only but also! Not only but also!

(Puts on <u>Light my Fire</u>)

PEGGY. That's fabulous.

(They dance. Doorbell)

BASIL. Go and open, honeybunch!

LADY DE M. I'm just putting on some makeup! You go!

BASIL. (calls) Step inside!

RICHARDS. (enters) And how is our great maestro this
evening?

BASIL. I welcome you with body and soul! Help yourself to
whisky.

RICHARDS. Just what I need. I've been working myself to
death over some idiotic article.

BASIL. This is Peggy. Come and join us, Hugh. We've
just met at the hospital.

(RICHARDS joins in the dance)

RICHARDS. Been to the hospital? To see Frank?

BASIL. Yes. It was most enjoyable. A most enjoyable
evening. Georgie got rid of her baby at the same time.
Yeah...all very successful.

RICHARDS. How come?

BASIL. Well, Frank pulled a few punches and the baby
didn't like it.

RICHARDS. You don't say.

BASIL. Oh yes...Frank is feeling a lot better now. He may

be coming round later.

RICHARDS. I'd be surprised if he dared enter the lion's den.

BASIL. It's a bit of a drag without Frankie. (Pulling PEGGY closer) Peggy, my sweet!

RICHARDS. Where's your lovely wife?

BASIL. She's dressing up for you, Hugh. You'll have to watch it tonight, she's out to get you...

RICHARDS. I've got lots of energy to use up after writing that article.

(LADY DE MARLIMONT appears in the door, all dolled up)

LADY DE M. May I join in?

PEGGY. That's the end of the record.

BASIL. You come in and the record stops.

LADY DE M. Don't tell me it's my fault that the record is finished.

(She puts the record on again, dances up to RICHARDS, they dance in a clinch. ANTOINE enters with a bottle of whisky in his hand)

ANTOINE. Who cometh walking upon the wind
And riding high upon the storm
It is Antoine - the wiggly worm.

(Laughs piercingly) Let me kiss you, beloved!

BASIL. Hello there, old ass.

ANTOINE. Hello, hello, hello...a new face! Ah, that's without doubt a young Okapi. That's something very special indeed.

BASIL. (to PEGGY) If you think he's soft in the head you're

mistaken. The gentleman is perfectly normal.

PEGGY. I'm not so sure.

ANTOINE. Okapis are never quite sure, remember that.
Even the Good Lord was not quite sure what sort of an
animal to create...even the Good Lord had his doubts
on that score!

BASIL. Where have you been all this time?

ANTOINE. In my own little room. Yes, I've been sitting in
my own little room, discussing the theory of mysticism
with Mama...

(PEGGY giggles)

There's nothing to laugh about Okapi. Things are somewhat complex...they couldn't get any complex-er!
Cheers, my lord!

BASIL. Cheers, you old philosophizer!

(FRANK enters in dressing gown and pyjamas)

FRANK. Hello, everyone!

(He seems gayer and more cheerful)

BASIL. Frank, my dearest! Look who's here, everybody!

RICHARDS. Been to a pyjama party?

PEGGY. If the house surgeon gets to know about this!
You're supposed to stay in bed another week.

BASIL. He can stay in bed wherever he is! Have a drink,
mate!

FRANK. Thanks. You know, I'm so glad to be out of that
bloody hospital.

PEGGY. How's your lady friend?

FRANK. They say she's better.

BASIL. Still cross that we came?

FRANK. No, but you know, being in hospital and all that, Georgie really got on my nerves with all that fuss.

BASIL. She was a bit on the fatty side. Now then, everybody. We're all together again, one large family!

FRANK. What I find is amazing is that I keep coming back to you.

BASIL. You're our yoyo, or whatever it's called.

FRANK. That's what I feel like. But what can I do...a game's a game. And without a game to play I can't exist. Now I feel all right again for the first time in ages.

BASIL. I suppose it was that liberating blow.

FRANK. Maybe you're right.

ANTOINE. I'm telling you hedgehog: it's important to be with it, not just on the edge of things...and the readiness is all, as the great bard so perceptively remarked.

(FRANK puts on a rock record, laughs, starts to dance)

BASIL. (laughs) Rock! Rock!

(He starts to rock wildly with PEGGY. ANTOINE dances by himself making boxer-like movements. RICHARDS dances with LADY DE MARLIMONT quickly reaching a euphoric state)

All change!

(He pushes PEGGY towards FRANK and dances with ANTOINE)

All change!

94

(He dances with his wife, FRANK with RICHARDS, and PEGGY with ANTOINE)

All change!

(BASIL takes off his top, takes PEGGY's sweater, they exchange clothes)

All change!

(The others do the same)

All change. Rock!

(Dancing continues with varying changes - hectic dressing and undressing and calls of 'All change'. At the end they are exhausted and make for the whisky bottles)

LADY DE M. Phhooo, I'm hot! I must have a drink.

PEGGY. Let's put it on again!

FRANK. I'm going to sit this one out.

BASIL. Have a drink.

FRANK. Fill it up then. (Drinks)

RICHARDS. No more rock for me...or else I'll go home and finish writing my article.

FRANK. What are you writing about?

RICHARDS. Basil.

FRANK. What about Basil?

RICHARDS. A comparison with Stubbs.

BASIL. I'm a great admirer of Stubbs. Listen, I'll tell you what we're going to do now! We're going to play the game of total change!

RICHARDS. You can count me out.

LADY DE M. Me too.

BASIL. We'll see. You don't have to dance. This is how it goes.

(Makes a movement as if to throw away his own body)

Everybody throws away his own stinking body and takes someone else's stinking body.

RICHARDS. Okay. My clean body won't be able to take part.

BASIL. Antoine is going to be Mum...

LADY DE M. Stop calling me Mum...

BASIL. Antoine is my wife, and my wife is Antoine. Hugh is...let's say...the late Air Vice Marshal, Peggy is someone she knows...

PEGGY. Mr. Middleton!

BASIL. Frank is me and I am Frank!

LADY DE M. And what's all that supposed to mean?

BASIL. Just a game to while away the time, Mummy dear.

ANTOINE. Splendid. I am the llama!

BASIL. That's it.

ANTOINE. 'We'll gather lilacs in the spring again...'

FRANK. (laughs) That's great. Basil you're really getting to be something.

BASIL. Basil is a genius!

RICHARDS. What about me? What am I supposed to do? Call The Pope?

BASIL. Certainly.

RICHARDS. The Pope...the Pope...Whore! Tart!...
Who is that man...who is that man?

(Everyone is amused)

BASIL. And you are Antoine, Mama.

LADY DE M. Go on.

ANTOINE. You are my former body, llama!

LADY DE M. What, do you want me to call him llama?

BASIL. You've got it pussycat!

PEGGY. May I try Mr. Middleton?

BASIL. But of course, beautiful! (Puts on slow record)
Right. Take your seats. Fasten your seatbelts!

(They sit in a circle, drink and smoke)

BASIL. All change! I should like to point out that this is my
own invention, copyright reserved.

FRANK. A kind of parlour game.

BASIL. Nonsense. Parlour game - I wouldn't want to take part
in anything as obscene, would I, Mum? Play forfeits with
car keys or strip poker or other such childish things...
oh no. The All Change game is different...it's a serious
game and has nothing to do with sex or the erotic.

ANTOINE. It's quite a remarkable game.

BASIL. The important thing is to look each other in the eye.

FRANK. Stare each other out.

BASIL. If you like, okay. (To FRANK, speaking as FRANK)
You know, you ought to read a bit, Basil...it's all
very well to be naive, but...you know...you must
become more relaxed. Read Molloy for instance, or

97

Joyce. (They all look at FRANK)

FRANK. That's another of those tricks like the one with the fairy tale.

BASIL. A first warning, Frank.

ANTOINE. What was that about a fairy tale? I wasn't there, slickety pig. (Looks at FRANK)

BASIL. (to ANTOINE) You know, we were reading fairy tales, Mrs. O'Malley, and I...I had to read aloud. But I couldn't read so well...

RICHARDS. The Pope...the Pope! (Rises, walks about. Points to FRANK) Who is that? Who is that? (To ANTOINE) You whore, you...Brothel Madam! She's fucking, the old sow!

ANTOINE. That's not true, Charles...it's not true!

LADY DE M. I don't like you making jokes about Charles.

BASIL. (to her) Antoine! Don't pinch me. Don't pinch me, jellyfish! Listen, Antoine, how about helping a bit with building up Basil...help him along a bit...you know, build him up...and then drop him.

LADY DE M. (laughs) Splendid! Absolutely diabolical, Basil!

BASIL. Not Basil, I am Frank.

LADY DE M. Hedgehog...

(RICHARDS walks about talking to himself)

PEGGY. Oh, I've got a temperature...I feel so ill...

ANTOINE. (moves to FRANK) Basil, my love, come into the room next door. It's your marital duty, Basil.

BASIL. (to ANTOINE) No, pussycat, he's got to be made to loosen up a bit first, you know, pussycat...listen to jazz, read Beckett...

(They all look at FRANK)

FRANK. (to himself) Okay, I'll join in.

LADY DE M. Slickety pig is going to join in.

FRANK. (to BASIL) You know, Frank, all your wisdom is
a lot of shit. If you wanted to build me up you've
slipped up, boyo. I've heard it all from Georgie or
whatever her name is. I slept with her in the kitchen
the other night.

BASIL. Okay, okay...that's great. Couldn't be better. It's
fantastic, that fits perfectly into my plan.

ANTOINE. (to FRANK) Basil darling, tell us the story
about the reception.

FRANK. (draining a glass of whisky) Go on, how many more
times am I supposed to tell?

ANTOINE. Tell us...

FRANK. Well, they were all lining up, as if they were
queuing outside the breadshop and pressed the Minister's
clammy hand...so I said: Bon soir, Monsieur. The
Minister replies: Bon soir, Monsieur. So I say: Oh,
I've made a mistake...I am British...

(They laugh)

LADY DE M. Great, slickety pig!

BASIL. Tell us how you stripped!

FRANK. Well, I just took my clothes off...you see...the
Minister was talking about the eternal redeeming
message of art...and he got more and more red in
the face...

ANTOINE. Like you, my love! (Kisses FRANK)

LADY DE M. (to BASIL) Hedgehog dearest, read us a
     fairy tale!

BASIL. Oh, no, I don't know. It's a bit childish. I don't
     know...I don't know.

ANTOINE. (taking a book from the shelf, to BASIL) Read,
     Frank!

FRANK. Looks a pretty boring story.

BASIL. (fending off) No...I don't want to read now. I
     sense trouble.

ANTOINE. Go on, read!

LADY DE M. Diabolical!

RICHARDS. The Pope...(To ANTOINE) Whore, tart, etc.

BASIL. All right then. ('Reading') The Tale of the Little
     Tree. ...shall I go on?

ANTOINE. Read on!

BASIL. Once upon a time, there lived a man and his wife
     and they had a little tree. (Breathing heavily)...they
     had a little tree... (FRANK laughs hysterically)...
     in a beautiful garden. But the tee...eh, eh...the
     tree didn't want to stay...eh, eh...stand against the
     wind and the weather. It gave them much trouble...
     they replanted it. But it would not go...eh, eh...
     grow that tee...eh...No, I can't read now. (Rises)
     I must go...I feel sick.

     (FRANK laughs hysterically)

ANTOINE. (to RICHARDS) I'm good, Charles...

RICHARDS. No! You're lyyying! Whore! You're de-
     ceiving me with the Pope!

     (They laugh)

ANTOINE. No, with Basil.

RICHARDS. (pretending to collapse) Eeeeeehhhh! (Drops
    to the ground)

    (GEORGIE enters, she is still weak, goes straight up
    to BASIL, falls into his arms and cries)

LADY DE M. Georgie, darling!

FRANK. (jumps to his feet) There she goes again! Crying
    again! My God! Christ, how mixed up you are! I'm
    telling you, believe me! I'm telling you. (Goes to
    record player, puts on rock number) Up you get, you
    lame ducks, we're going to dance! All change! (To
    ANTOINE) Come here, pussycat! Come to me! Kiss
    my toes!

    (ANTOINE kisses his feet)

ANTOINE. But don't hit me, Basil my love!

RICHARDS. (rising) The Pope... (To ANTOINE) You whore
    ...you common slut!

FRANK. Let's dance, everybody.

    (Pulls PEGGY towards him)

    (During this scene BASIL and GEORGIE sit in an arm-
    chair. They are tenderly in love which in turn, causes
    an artificial euphoria. The others rock and scream)

LADY DE M. Slickety pig. Come dance with me. Llama!
    Llama!

ANTOINE. We'll gather lilacs in the spring again... Rock,
    rock.

    All change.

RICHARDS. The Pope... Pope - rock... Whore - rock...

FRANK. (to PEGGY) Rock, midget, rock... or are your bones dried up to dust!

PEGGY. Not so tight.

FRANK. Not so tight. You're going to get to know me, little mouse.

(Shakes her brutally)

PEGGY. Stop it! (Tries to break away)

FRANK. (pulls her back) You stay here with your Uncle Basil!

PEGGY. Outch!

FRANK. (falls upon her and to the ground) Here and now! Here and now! (The others dance around them) Here and now!

ALL. Here and now!

PEGGY. Let me go! Basil! Basil!

(BASIL kisses GEORGIE. RICHARDS falls to the ground crying: The Pope. ANTOINE clings to FRANK, calling: Basil, my love. PEGGY scratches FRANK)

FRANK. Outch!

(PEGGY frees herself, picks up her coat and runs out of the room. The record is finished. They breathe heavily and relax. FRANK lights a cigarette and goes out of the room)

RICHARDS. Let's open the window, it's too hot in here.

LADY DE M. Don't bother, Hugh, I'll do it.

(She opens a large window. Rain and sleet is falling

and gales are blowing outside. RICHARDS, ANTOINE
and LADY DE M walk about breathing heavily, wiping
their foreheads and drinking. BASIL comforts
GEORGIE)

BASIL. It's all right, my little pussy, my little...it's all
right.

GEORGIE. Can I have something to drink?

BASIL. There you are.

GEORGIE. No, not alcohol...wait a minute, I'll get some
water.

BASIL. I'll get you some...

GEORGIE. No, it's all right.

(She goes out. They sit and stare)

BASIL. An enjoyable evening, don't you think?

RICHARDS. Not bad.

(LADY DE MARLIMONT falls asleep in her chair)

ANTOINE. A diabolical evening. (Goes to the window, calls
into the wind)
Blow, blow thou winter wind -
Shall I compare thee to a summer's day...

(RICHARDS turns off centre light)

BASIL. Fresh air is the best drink...

(ANTOINE plays an excerpt from the Storm Scene in
King Lear, then sits. LADY DE MARLIMONT begins
to snore. For some time only snoring is heard. Then
a short cry from GEORGIE. She appears in the door)

GEORGIE. It's Frank!

BASIL. What's the matter?

(GEORGIE indicates hanging)

BASIL. (cries) He's hanged himself?

GEORGIE. In the loo.

(For some time only snoring is heard, then BASIL goes up to LADY DE MARLIMONT and holds her nose. She wakes up gasping for breath)

THE END

PARTY FOR SIX

CHARACTERS

FERDINAND
FRED
FRANK
FLOSSIE
FREDA
LANDLORD
FANNY

SCENE ONE

(Entrance Hall. Open door to Lounge on Left. Door
to Passage upstage. In the centre of the floor a large,
heavy carpet. A ceiling light, bright and cold when lit
up. Upstage Right in the corner, a hat and coat stand.
On the wall Right a cupboard with built-in drinks
cabinet. Between cupboard and hat and coat stand an
old discarded divan, grey and shabby. When the
curtain rises the Hall is almost in darkness. The only
source of light is through the open Lounge door.
Sound of pop records and clinking of glasses from the
Lounge. FERDINAND, a student aged 20, enters
from the Lounge turns the light on in the Hall, goes
to Drinks cabinet, takes out some bottles of wine,
turns the light off and disappears back into the Lounge
clinking his bottles. He returns, turns on the light,
takes a bunch of keys from a hook by the door to
passage at back and goes out into the passage. The
stage remains light. After some time he enters from
back. Sound of water flushing lavatory. He turns off
the light, goes into the Lounge and closes the door.
The stage is now in complete darkness. In the Lounge
FERDY puts on another record: Come Prima. It is
heard softly through the door. Doorbell. FERDY
enters from Lounge, turns on light, goes through door
to passage and, outside, opens another door. Voices:)

FERDY'S VOICE. Hi.

FRED. Hello there.

FERDY. Come on in.

FRED. Anyone here yet?

FERDY. No, you're the first. (They enter Hall) Got the
brandy?

FRED. Yeah. I've got some. Pinched it from my old lady.

FERDY. Great.

FRED. I could have got some more...but...

FERDY. (disappearing into the Lounge) Take your things
off. Just going to bung on another record.

FRED. (takes off his coat, puts bottle on divan) Hey!
Ferdy! Ferdy!

FERDY. (putting on record) Yeah? What's up?

FRED. Is Frank going to bring some booze too?

FERDY. He said he would.

FRED. Is Fanny coming?

FERDY. Shut up. Listen to my new record.

FRED. Is Fanny coming?

FERDY. (entering from Lounge) Listen to that record.
(Sings) If I had...

FRED. Hey! Is Fanny coming?

FERDY. (his attention on record) Yeah. Sure. Come on
inside. Leave the booze there for now. We'll kick
off with beer. (Both go into the room. FERDY turns
off the light in the Hall. FRED is about to close the
door...only their Voices are heard:)

FERDY'S VOICE. Leave the door open. Or we won't hear
the bell. Great record, isn't it?

FRED'S VOICE. Not bad.

FERDY. Bought it yesterday. (They appear to be listening to record as nothing else is heard. When the record finishes:)

FRED'S VOICE. Is it true that Frank has taken up with Fanny?

FERDY. That's what he says. But I think...

FRED. I always thought it was no go with her.

FERDY. On the contrary. If you give her the right soft soap you're in clover with her. But I don't know if Frank...

FRED. That's what I mean.

FERDY. I don't believe it. Anyway. You got your eye on her?

FRED. What do you mean 'got my eye on her'. I was just wondering. Might have a bit of a go tonight.

FERDY. What about Flossie?

FRED. Don't you want her?

FERDY. I don't want anybody in particular. I'll make do with Fanny if necessary.

FRED. And Frank?

FERDY. He can have Freda. (Laughs)

FRED. You don't know Frank.

FERDY. It'll sort itself out. Wait and see. (Doorbell is rung repeatedly) I'll go. Put on a good record.

(FERDY enters Hall and turns on the light. FRED puts on the same record as before. FERDY out to Passage and opens the door. Voices:)

FERDY. In you come!

FLOSSIE. Hi.

FERDY. Hi there!

FRANK. Hello. Anybody here yet?

FERDY. No. (Enters) Come on in. Close the door after you, please. Freddie's here.

FRED. (from Lounge) Hello!

FRANK. Hi, mate!

FRED. How's the old boozer.

FERDY. Take your things off.

FLOSSIE. (FERDY takes her coat) Thanks. (FRANK has taken his coat off and goes into the Lounge) Got a mirror somewhere?

FRANK. (in Lounge) Hello.

FERDY. You look smashing as you are. (FLOSSIE giggles) Come on. (They go into the Lounge. FERDY turns off light in the Hall. The door remains open and some light falls into the Hall. Their VOICES only:)

FLOSSIE. (apparently to FRED) Hello.

FERDY. Have you heard this record?

FRANK. This one?

FERDY. Hang on. I'll play it again.

FRED. Play something else. We can have it after.

FERDY. No. Hang on. Just a second.

FLOSSIE. I'd like to hear this one.

FERDY. This one?

FLOSSIE. Or this.

FERDY. Oh, wait a mintue. Let's play this one first. Then
you can play what you like. (Puts on record, turns
volume right up. Sings)

FRED. Turn it down a bit! (Volume very low)

FLOSSIE. I thought Freda and Fanny would be here...

FERDY. Well, as you see...

FLOSSIE. Am I the only female here then...(Smiles audibly)

FRED. (slily) So far! So far...let's hope...let's hope
some more will turn up! (Laughs. Long pause. Very
long pause, then someone (FRANK) closes the door.
The stage is plunged in darkness and all is quiet.
After some time the door is opened)

FERDY. Just in case. So we can hear the bell. (Pause)

FLOSSIE. I wonder where they've got to.

FRED. All in good time.

FRANK. (laughs a little) Good time - you don't say!

FLOSSIE. D'you mind if I help myself to one of these?

FERDY. Help yourself! Have some eats while it's there.

   (Pause while they eat)

FRANK. What's that?

FERDY. I don't know. It all came in a packet.

FLOSSIE. It's a bit like...what d'you call it...a cheese-straw.

FERDY. There's cheese in it.

FRED. Not bad. (FRANK goes to door and into the dark
Hall)

111

FRANK. Where's the light?

FERDY. (calls from the room) To the right of the door. To the right.

(FRANK turns on light)

FRANK. Is there a key?

FERDY. No. By the other door. There's a whole bunch of them.

FRANK. Got it. (Goes out to Passage, leaves light on in Hall)

FRED. How about opening one of these bottles?

FERDY. Shouldn't we wait until everyone's here?

FLOSSIE. I don't mind. I don't really want a drink.

FRED. I wouldn't mind a beer.

FERDY. Help yourself if you want one...

(Sound of bottles)

FRED. Got a bottle opener?

FERDY. Isn't there one there? (Pause)

FRED. Can't see one.

FERDY. (enters Hall and goes to drinks cabinet, searches, muttering) Shit...where's the bottle opener? (Finds one. Goes back into Lounge, leaves light on in Hall) Here you are!

FRED. Thanks. (Sound of bottle being opened) Shall I open another one?

FERDY. Not for me.

FRED. What about you?

FLOSSIE. No thanks. I'll just have a nibble.

FERDY. Good, aren't they.

FLOSSIE. Super. Where did you get them?

FERDY. I don't know what the place is called. At the top of Market Street.

FLOSSIE. Keen's?

FERDY. Where's that?

FLOSSIE. Next to Horne's.

FERDY. Where's Horne's?

FRED. Opposite the stamp shop.

FERDY. Yeah, that's it. Yeah.

FLOSSIE. That's where I do my shopping. (FRANK comes back into the Hall. Sound of water flushing)

FRANK. Shall I turn the light off?

FERDY. Yes, turn it off. (FRANK turns off light, goes into Lounge, closes the door, opens it again at once)

FRANK. You having a beer?

FERDY. Like one?

FRANK. What a question. Let's have it. Now we're away!

(FRED laughs in agreement)

FERDY. Great minds think.alike, eh?

FRANK. Cheers.

FRED. Bottoms up! (Soon both exclaim with exaggerated delight: Aaahhhh!)

FERDY. I think I'll have one too. What have you done with the bottle opener?

FRED. Here you are. (Doorbell)

FLOSSIE. That'll be them.

FERDY. I'll go... (Enters Hall, turns on light, goes out to Passage. Voices:)

(FERDY makes sound of a fanfare. Opens door. FANNY and FREDA laugh)

Hello to you!

FANNY. Hello to you, he says! (Laughs)

FREDA. Are we last.

FERDY. Yeah. (Shows them in) Come on in!

(Someone puts on a new record in the Lounge. Volume fairly high)

Take your coats off! (He takes coats. FLOSSIE enters from Lounge)

FLOSSIE. Hello.

FREDA. Hello, Flossie.

FANNY. Been here long?

FLOSSIE. No, I've only just come.

FANNY. Christ! I think I've left my comb behind!

FLOSSIE. You don't need one.

FERDY. You look smashing as you are.

FREDA. (whispers to FERDY) Where's the loo?

CURTAIN

SCENE TWO

(The same as in Scene One. The Hall is lit up. The
door to the Lounge is closed, music is heard from
inside. FRED is standing in the Hall, he looks undecided as if waiting for something. Outside the
lavatory is flushed. FANNY enters, hangs up the key
on the hook by the passage door. FRED quickly moves
up to her from behind, embraces her and kisses the
back of her neck. She struggles free)

FANNY. Mind my dress.

FRED. Don't go.

FANNY. What do you want? (FRED gives her a juicy kiss)
    Ha! (FANNY goes into Lounge and closes the door
    after her. FRED takes the bunch of keys and goes
    out through door to passage. He is somewhat tipsy.
    For a time the Hall remains empty. Then:)

FERDY. (looking out from Lounge) Freddie? Freddie?

FRED. (muffled) Engaged.

FERDY. (into Lounge) (laughs) Engaged! (Laughter rings
    out from the Lounge, FERDY closes the door)

FRED. (sings) Lalala lalala lalala! A-hunting we will go
    ...Lalala lalala lalala (Flushes)

(FRED enters Hall, hangs up keys, goes to Lounge
door and listens. He turns off the light, and turns it
on again. On, off, on, off. Nearly twenty times.
With the light on he knocks on the Lounge door.
Several voices call: 'Come in'. FRED goes into the
Lounge)

FLOSSIE. Oh, it's you?

FRED. Go on! You didn't expect me!

    (VOICES:)

FERDY. Freda, put on a twist record!

FRANK. Twist Twist, Twist, Twist!

FERDY. Shut the door somebody! (The door is slammed shut, the stage remains lit up and empty. The sound of music is low. Gradually it increases. The noise of the party in the Lounge reaches its climax. Laughter. Doorbell. The noise in the Lounge stops. FERDY opens the door. VOICES:)

FLOSSIE. I didn't hear anything.

FRANK. I thought I did. (Doorbell is rung again)

FANNY. I expect it's the landlord. (FERDY crosses Hall and goes out into the Passage. He opens the door. Voices:)

FERDY. Good evening.

LANDLORD'S VOICE. Tell me, Mr. P., have you got a zoo full of monkeys in there?

(Laughter from the Lounge)

FERDY. No.

LANDLORD. That's what it sounds like. I think the whole house is coming down. It is quite unbearable.

FERDY. I do apologise. We'll be quiet in a minute. You know, we've got a little party going...

LANDLORD. Okay. I've got nothing against parties. But you don't have to go stamping around all the time.

FERDY. No, no. That was only just now. We were playing a game of forfeits, you know. And we got a bit carried away.

LANDLORD. All right, all right. But try and keep it bearable - please.

FERDY. Cheerio!

LANDLORD. Good night. (FERDY closes the door)

FERDY. (in the Hall) Carry on, everybody. (Goes back into the Lounge) No need for restraint. The landlord is quite sympathetic.

FRED. You don't say!

FREDA. Yeah! (The door remains slightly ajar)

FRANK. Anybody got a fag? (Several voices: No)

FANNY. I may have some in my coat pocket.

FRANK. Mind if I get them?

FANNY. Go ahead, in the left inside pocket.

(FRANK goes into the Hall and to coat stand. He looks through pockets)

FRANK. Where?

FANNY. The left inside pocket, or on the right outside.

(FRANK searches)

FRANK. Not a thing! (Goes back to Lounge door) You have a look.

FANNY. Oh, men are hopeless...

(Goes into the Hall and towards coat stand. FRANK closes Lounge door and turns the light off. For a short time nothing is seen or heard. Then heavy breathing. The Lounge door is opened abruptly. FLOSSIE looks into the Hall and turns on the light)

FLOSSIE. I beg your pardon! (They are sitting on the divan, somewhat embarrassed, but nothing much seems to have happened. FLOSSIE closes the door and turns the light off)

117

FANNY. Come on. Let's get back inside.

FRANK. Wait a bit. They want to be alone too.

FANNY. Come on. (FANNY turns on the light, straightens her hair. FRANK remains seated on the divan) Come on now.

(FANNY goes back into the Lounge, FRANK lies down on the divan. The Lounge door is slammed, the light stays on, FRANK closes his eyes. Soon the Lounge door is opened abruptly)

FERDY. There he is!

FRED'S VOICE. He's asleep.

FREDA. Frankie! Frankie! Wakey-wakey!

FRANK. Turn off that bloody light!

(They turn it off, return to the Lounge and close the door. For some time everything is quiet, then the Lounge door is opened again. FRED enters carrying a glass full of wine, turns on the light, goes over to the divan and pours the wine over FRANK's face)

FRANK. Bloody bastard! (He does not move. FRED runs back into the Lounge, giggling and somewhat frightened, and locks the door from inside)

CURTAIN

SCENE THREE

(The same. The Hall is brightly lit. FRANK is sleeping on the divan. The three girls' coats and FRED's duffle coat have gone from the hat and coat stand. The Lounge door is half open. For a long time there is no action. Then - somewhere, far away, the noise of goods waggons being shunted in a railway

yard. Then silence. Sound of shunting is repeated at
regular intervals (30 seconds). After four minutes -)

CURTAIN

SCENE FOUR

(The same. The Hall is brightly lit and empty. All
doors are wide open. FANNY enters from the passage,
wearing an overall. She is carrying clean glasses
which she replaces in the drinks cabinet)

FANNY. Not one of them broken. (Sound of vacuum
cleaner from the Lounge) It takes twice as long as
the party itself to clear up afterwards! (Goes back
into the passage)

FLOSSIE. It's not too bad. (Continues to hoover Lounge.
FANNY returns to the Hall carrying two clean plates.
She stops in the centre of the Hall, smiles in the
direction of the Lounge and calls out)

FANNY. Frank caught it bad last night!

FLOSSIE. (above the vacuum cleaner) And how! (FANNY
puts plates into drink cabinet)

CURTAIN

MAGIC AFTERNOON

CHARACTERS

BRIGIT
MONIKA
CHARLEY
JOE

(BRIGIT, MONIKA, CHARLEY and JOE are out of their
teens but trapped in a kind of identity-vacuum, neither
adolescents nor adults, uncommitted to anything.
Their behaviour projects a kind of constant put-on
which veils their desperate anomie, plus an empty
anxiety at having nothing worthwhile to be and nothing
interesting to do. These are potential 'true believers'
who have never found a leader and who have neither
the vitality nor the courage, nor even (any more) the
biological impulse to strike out into an existence as
mature human beings.

Scene: A sloppy bed-sitter in CHARLEY's bachelor flat.
The big unmade double-bed in the centre is scattered
with the detritus of a bored and pointless existence,
which litters the whole room: newspapers, 'serious'
paperbacks, of both classics and modern writers,
various underground publications, porn magazines,
tit magazines, especially Playboy, plus numerous LPs,
some in their sleeves, some not - the latest in pop
plus standards like Simon and Garfunkel, Dylan, Wilson
Pickett, John Coltrane, Roland Kirk, Shostakovich,
Beethoven, Vivaldi, Bach, etc. Among the records
and reading material is strewn a mess of dirty dishes,
empty booze and milk bottles, etc. There is a TV set,
a wardrobe, a stool or two, mats on the floor, chairs,
a gramophone, a small table with a dusty typewriter
on it, lamps, a large window at the back with venetian
blinds up, psychedelic-patterned drapes, and on the
obviously hand-painted walls are posters, pictures of
Mao, Che, etc., and perhaps a couple of C. Logue's
poster poems. There are exits to the kitchen, the
bathroom and hall. Outside, a beautiful summer after-

noon with sun pouring in through the window, birds
singing. In front of a large mirror CHARLEY and
BRIGIT are maneuvering. BRIGIT is examing the
effect of no bra and a thin T-shirt, CHARLEY trying
to comb his hair. They are sharing a cigarette.)

BRIGIT. (taking the cigarette from him) Why don't <u>you</u>
light one?

CHARLEY. (flops on the bed, looking for the packet) What
did you do with 'em?

BRIGIT. (suddenly curious, lifts up the T-shirt to expose
her breasts, peering into the mirror) Hey, did you
see this?

CHARLEY. (rooting in her handbag) Uh huh.

BRIGIT. Charley, look!

CHARLEY. (groping in her Levis hip pockets) Come on,
where did you put 'em?

BRIGIT. Charley, one is bigger than the other!

CHARLEY. (absently, looking for the cigarettes among the
trash) I know. It crosses over just a little. The left
one.

BRIGIT. (peering into the mirror) The left one?

CHARLEY. What did you do with the fags?

BRIGIT. What do you mean, crosses over?

CHARLEY. When you kiss me. Like this. (Crosses his
eyes)

BRIGIT. Not my eyes, my tits! You see? One is bigger
than the other!

CHARLEY. (finds the packet under the bed: empty) Shit!
You got the last one.

BRIGIT. (sighs, finds her jacket, takes a pack out of
the pocket, throws it to CHARLEY) What time is it?

CHARLEY. No idea. Two?

BRIGIT. What are we doing tonight? (Lights another
cigarette)

CHARLEY. No idea.

BRIGIT. It must be about three...I left at eleven...about
four hours...

CHARLEY. (picks up the phone, dials TIM) Two-thirty...
(Wanders around the room) peep...peep...peep...
at the third stroke it will be two-thirty and ten seconds
...peep peep peep... (Looking for a match to light his
cigarette) three-thirty...peep...four-thirty...peep
...five-thirty...peep... (Falsetto chant, imitating
the operator) the sands of time remorselessly run o -
on - peep...and o - on...peep peep...and o - on...
peep peep peep...

BRIGIT. (bored, has heard this before) So there's nothing
we can do tonight?

CHARLEY. I don't know. What do you want to do?

BRIGIT. I don't know. What do you want to do?

CHARLEY. Go for a walk?

BRIGIT. In this heat?

CHARLEY. Fuckall else we can do.

BRIGIT. What you mean is, you're broke again.

CHARLEY. Can't you get something from your mum?

BRIGIT. (she has heard this before) A quid, maybe two...
that won't take us very far.

CHARLEY. (picks up a gin bottle and drinks instead of

125

lighting his cigarette) Well, a couple of quid...

BRIGIT. (reaches for the bottle, but he keeps it) Can't you get some bread?

CHARLEY. Larry owes me a fiver...but he's out of town.

BRIGIT. (still wants the bottle) Come on, love... (Takes the bottle)

CHARLEY. Go swimming?

BRIGIT. I don't have my bikini.

CHARLEY. Who needs that old thing? (Leers unconvincingly)

BRIGIT. We could go to Eddie's. He's dying to show me his boat.

CHARLEY. He's dying to show you his cock. Anyway, the car's not ready yet.

BRIGIT. You mean you haven't paid them yet.

CHARLEY. Darling, I spent it all on you! (Pause) Stupid...

(Long pause)

BRIGIT. Stupider and stupider.

CHARLEY. Right.

BRIGIT. According to you.

CHARLEY. According to you. (Shakes himself all over) Aaaahhh!

BRIGIT. (sighs) Is there anything else to eat?

CHARLEY. Uuh...some bread, I think.

BRIGIT. Salami? No.

CHARLEY. (sighs) Ah...there must be something out there...

BRIGIT. (goes out to the kitchen, leaves the door open)
     There's something...it looks like cheese or something
     ...can I take that?

CHARLEY. Yeah...don't take it all. (Picks up a news-
     paper.

BRIGIT. (off) It tastes funny. How long have you had it?

CHARLEY. I don't know...couple of weeks, I guess.

BRIGIT. (spitting sounds) You bastard!

     (Comes in, washing out her mouth with gulps of tonic
     water, sprays it at him. CHARLEY protects himself
     with the newspaper)

     Whooo - the gin made me thirsty.

CHARLEY. (peeping over the edge of the newspaper) Fizz
     ...fizz...gin fizz.

BRIGIT. (empties the bottle, turns it upside down) Peace.
     (Settles behind CHARLEY, runs her fingers through
     his hair) Hey...you... (Pause)

CHARLEY. Hmmmmmm?

BRIGIT. Movies?

CHARLEY. Nothing.

BRIGIT. (takes the paper, points) What about that one?

CHARLEY. I saw the trailer. Catherine Deneuve and her
     flaccid thighs. Nothing.

BRIGIT. What about this one...

CHARLEY. Not to be missed...yech.

BRIGIT. I wouldn't mind seeing something...serious.

CHARLEY. Nobody's stopping you.

BRIGIT. But there isn't anything else!

CHARLEY. If I did go...ahhh... (Takes the paper) The Fight for The World Cup...

BRIGIT. If you go to that, you'll go by yourself.

CHARLEY. (languidly gives the paper back to her) Have another look. All I see is nothing.

BRIGIT. Gone With the Wind?

CHARLEY. Jesus, not again! Isn't there anything really... really shitty?

BRIGIT. At the Rialto...The Swedish Au Pair...

CHARLEY. Heeeyyy, right! Something really titty! Let's go!

BRIGIT. It's so far to the Rialto...

CHARLEY. (childish lisp) Can't I go to see the nasty mooovie?

BRIGIT. What about the Theatre?

CHARLEY. Whaaat? You want to go...to... (Affected tone) the theyuhtuh?

BRIGIT. Tomorrow there's King Lear again.

CHARLEY. (bored) Uh huh. And day after tomorrow?

BRIGIT. (leafing through the paper) It doesn't say...maybe it's in the week's events.

CHARLEY. (gets into bed) I'm going to sleep.

BRIGIT. (dropping the paper) You have any more jam... hey?

CHARLEY. Oh, have a look...but I'm not going down now ...not for that.

BRIGIT. (kneels on the bed, tickles him) Pleeease...
pretty please...nice jam...pretty please...with
<u>sugar</u> on it...nice jam? Nice Jam?

CHARLEY. (gives up, gets out of bed) What kind?

BRIGIT. Peach...or morello cherry!

CHARLEY. All they've got is black cherry and sour plum.

BRIGIT. Really nothing else?

CHARLEY. You've scoffed all the others.

BRIGIT. Then...sour plum. And see if there isn't something else. Morello cherry...

CHARLEY. (wearily) Okay... (He goes out)

BRIGIT. (puts on a record: Penny Lane. Looks at her
breasts in the mirror again, lifts her T-shirt. Then
has a thought and runs to the window) Charley!
Charley!

CHARLEY. (off) What?

BRIGIT. When was thalidomide invented?

CHARLEY. (off) Whaat?

BRIGIT. Never mind. Hurry up!

(Goes back to the mirror, lifts the T-shirt, weighs
each breast in a hand)

God! One is heavier, too!

(Begins to strike poses a la Playboy, unzips the fly
of her Levis, the poses become more and more ridiculous, she becomes rather excited with herself. She
begins to make faces to go with the poses, sticking
her lips out, licking them, etc. One of the poses
proves difficult. She gets a slight crick in her back
and tries again)

129

Damn...how do they do it?

(She tries, but it's not quite right. She tries something else and that's better. Tries uncovering one breast and then the other, then both, then pulling down the T-shirt tightly over her breasts. She reaches out and strokes the mirror lustfully)

De-licious!

(Turns her back to the mirror, pulls down the Levis to expose her bum. She espies a spot)

Oh, hell!

(She tries to squeeze the spot, but the location is awkward)

Tch...shit!

(She manages at last, examines the result on her fingernail and flicks it away. Then she looks longingly at herself over her shoulder and blows a kiss at the mirror. The telephone rings. Pulls Levis up and T-shirt down and goes to the window)

Charley! Shall I answer the phone?

CHARLEY. (off) Leave it!

BRIGIT. Why not?

(Heavy steps on the stairs)

CHARLEY. (entering with the jam) Let it ring.

BRIGIT. But why?

CHARLEY. Oh, Jesus, answer it, then...

BRIGIT. (picks up the phone) Hello? Hi! Uh huh...just fine... (Hands the receiver to CHARLEY)

CHARLEY. Yeah...hey, man! Yeah. Fuckall, man. Nah,

fuckall. Uh huh. Uh huh. Yeah. Just sitting here.
Yeah. Mama is away. Yeah. When? Crazy. Tonight.
Tonight, man. Nothing so far. We thought about the
mooovies. Only thing is...right. No bread. Right.
Hey! Yeah, man, I don't care. Uh huh. We're almost
out of booze. Gin. If you...yeah...uh huh...uh huh
...uh huh...right. Right. Yeah. Yeah...yeah.
Yeah. Naturally! Maybe if...okay...okay...yeah...
yeah...who, you? How do you mean? Yeah...always
the same, yeah...hey! (Laughs) Right. Uh-uh. Uh-
uh...you come here...sure...yeah...uh huh...yeah
...yeah...yeah...yeah...yeah...yeah...eeyeah!
Cheers.

(Hangs up)

BRIGIT. Is he coming?

CHARLEY. Maybe.

BRIGIT. What's he doing tonight?

CHARLEY. They dunno yet. Probably fuckall. (Turns out
his pocket and shakes it) They don't have any bread,
either.

BRIGIT. You really want to go out with them?

CHARLEY. Well, we're not doing anything. I dunno, maybe
a jar or two somewhere...

BRIGIT. I'm so tired...

CHARLEY. So sleep a little...

BRIGIT. I can't, not now.

CHARLEY. Nervous?

BRIGIT. No...not specially...

CHARLEY. Take a pill.

BRIGIT. I already took two today. You want one?

CHARLEY. It'd make me jittery.

BRIGIT. You're right, I'll take one more...just one...I
wanted to take one, that's why I got the lemonade...

(CHARLEY puts on a Wilson Pickett LP, turns it up,
but not quite high enough to drown the dialogue. With
a sudden spurt of energy he hops and moves around
the room, singing with the music)

BRIGIT. (sourly) You're all right, aren't you?

(No answer. He drums on the table and dances)

BRIGIT. (louder) I can't stand that Wilson Pickett any more!

CHARLEY. You just don't dig him yet!

BRIGIT. Ha, ha.

CHARLEY. (putting on the style) Heyy...I'm livin' again!
(Laughing maliciously) Don't need nothin' else...
(Smirking, spins away from her)

BRIGIT. (trying to chill his exuberance) Don't you have
anything I can read?

CHARLEY. (picks up a book as he dances, pitches it to her)
Norman Mailer...

BRIGIT. (letting the book fall at her feet) He's a bore...
(CHARLEY ignores her. She says it louder) He's a
BORE... (Kicks the book under the bed)

CHARLEY. You flipped, or what? (Singing, drumming
again, he picks up another book from the table) The
de-VINE...MarQUIIIIIS - (Spins past her, drops the
books in her lap)

BRIGIT. (picks up the book goes to the gram, turns it down
a bit) De Sade... (With a bored air, opens the book
and reads sarcastically) ...and I discharged upon
her...and I discharged upon her... (Turns a page)
...and I discharged upon her... (Turns a page) ...

and I discharged upon her... (Sighs) A little mono-
tonous, isn't it? (Drops the book on the floor)

CHARLEY. (still dancing, crooning the music) I told you,
read the Norman Mailer! It's good!

BRIGIT. The great American statue who's seen a lot of
pigeons. No, thanks. (Smirking at him) You could
write something...for a change...

CHARLEY. Not while the mu-sic's going, man...oooo...
listen to that... (Drums again) Tatatata... (In rhythm)
Watcha want me to write...watcha want me to write...
write...write...write...

BRIGIT. You're an idle bastard.

CHARLEY. Listen, listen...I'll write a play...two people
on the stage...listening to records...one record...
and then another record... (Drums again)

BRIGIT. Ha, ha.

CHARLEY. And right there... (Points) Is this professor...
with a biig diagram of the...the nervous system...
right? And he's explaining what the music...does to
it...right? And he's sort of singing what he says...
like it was set to music...

BRIGIT. You don't have a single idea, do you?

CHARLEY. (stung) Maybe you should write the fucking play.

BRIGIT. Maybe I should.

CHARLEY. I've got plenty of ideas.

BRIGIT. All you've got is bullshit.

CHARLEY. Hey, you're right...you know you're right?
Cause everything is bullshit...

BRIGIT. Oh, sure...

CHARLEY. Life is a habit...like smoking cigarettes!

BRIGIT. I've heard that before...it's one of your bullshit poems.

CHARLEY. (sits at the typewriter, flicks off the gram, blows the dust off the machine) What about this...the driving force in this world...is constipation! Whatever way you turn it...it's still a lot of shit!

(BRIGIT clucks and closes her eyes in disgust)

Wait a minute, what about this? If you wanta make it, man...you do as little as possible...as fast as possible...

BRIGIT. It doesn't even rhyme.

CHARLEY. Blank verse!

BRIGIT. It's blank, all right. Shouldn't you exercise your brilliant intellect on the problem of what we're going to do tonight?

CHARLEY. I'm staying in...I'll get some writing done...

BRIGIT. You can write now!

CHARLEY. (shrugs, gets up) Ahh, I dunno...

BRIGIT. (irritated) But of course you'll know tonight...

CHARLEY. Sure, sure...

BRIGIT. Why'm I always so tired...I could sleep all day...

CHARLEY. All right, so sleep! Or go out and do some work or something...

BRIGIT. I can't even think about working...impossible... I mean, I feel all right, but I just don't want to do anything...

CHARLEY. Oh, don't be such a drag!

BRIGIT. What do you want? I can't do anything about it!

CHARLEY. So I'm a drag, too, right?

BRIGIT. Dunno. I mean, you don't give a shit about me.

CHARLEY. Yeah, well, unfortunately, I do. That's what knocks me out.

BRIGIT. Oh, sure.

CHARLEY. No, really!

BRIGIT. (mocks him) Really!

CHARLEY. Hey, let's go for a walk...

BRIGIT. You go. I'll stay here.

CHARLEY. Oh, cute. Very cute.

BRIGIT. Or maybe I'll go home.

CHARLEY. What for?

BRIGIT. Just lay around, I guess...

(She is on the bed. CHARLEY lies down beside her, embraces her)

BRIGIT. (fends him off) No...I don't feel like fucking, either...

CHARLEY. So drink something then. (Stung again, gets up and puts another LP on, something slow)

BRIGIT. God, we can't keep this up!

CHARLEY. But we are keeping it up...or are we?

BRIGIT. I don't even want to kill myself any more...I mean ...somehow I feel...I feel really good... (Pause) I don't look so bad today, do I?

CHARLEY. Like a real tart.

BRIGIT. Thank you very much.

CHARLEY. Slick, and smooth, and bright, and merry, and gay...

BRIGIT. God, you are stupid...

(CHARLEY goes out of the room)

BRIGIT. Where you going?

CHARLEY. The bog.

BRIGIT. Don't get any ideas in there...

CHARLEY. (melodramatic voice) Do not deceive me while I am away...

BRIGIT. What difference would it make to you? (Pause) When'd Joe say he was coming?

CHARLEY. What?

BRIGIT. When is Joe coming?

CHARLEY. He didn't say. (Pause) Hey! It's gonna rain. The clouds are as black as a witch's bum out there.

BRIGIT. I still want to go out tonight...

CHARLEY. We'll see. (Toilet flushes. He comes in) I do believe, there's gonna be a storm.

BRIGIT. Charley, when did Joe say he was coming?

CHARLEY. If he's coming, it won't be long.

BRIGIT. With Monika? Or not?

CHARLEY. Don't ask me...if they haven't had a fight, I suppose he'll bring Monika. (Goes to the window) Come the first of July, I am pissing off to Spain...whatever happens.

BRIGIT. And what am I supposed to do?

CHARLEY. Come along...

BRIGIT. Oh, sure...beautiful...and who'll pay the fare? Not mummy, that's for sure.

CHARLEY. Something'll turn up. Your old lady ought to give you something...she's got enough bloody bread...

BRIGIT. Turn up from where, I'd like to know...at least you'll have the car, I hope.

CHARLEY. Yeah, I hope...I'm not bloody hitching...

BRIGIT. Why not?

CHARLEY. Do me a favour.

BRIGIT. You're just too fucking idle...

CHARLEY. Sure.

BRIGIT. Well, you are!

CHARLEY. Okay, I'm too fucking idle... (Yawns)

(Outside, a car goes by)

BRIGIT. That could be Joe!

CHARLEY. (goes to the window) Uh-uh.

BRIGIT. (smugly) But it was a Volkswagen.

CHARLEY. (quiz show manner) Give that lady a big... black...CIGAR! Now would you like to try for some-thing...mmmm...nicer?

BRIGIT. Hey...does Joe know you've been fucking Monika?

CHARLEY. Uh huh. He more or less knows what's going on.

BRIGIT. Of course you told him...

CHARLEY. Of course.

BRIGIT. God, you're like a couple of old biddies, gossiping over the back fence!

CHARLEY. So? So we talk over things for a couple of hours? (Pause) It's sort of interesting the way all these little things get around...

BRIGIT. Madly.

CHARLEY. Everybody tangled up with everybody else...ha!

BRIGIT. (pause) Christ, I'll be glad to get out of this shit-bag!

CHARLEY. You're not the only one.

BRIGIT. Jesus, I've got to pee again...

CHARLEY. I vote we stay in tonight...

BRIGIT. Well, we'll just see...I wouldn't count on it... (Goes out)

(A clap of thunder outside)

CHARLEY. There she goes! (Calls) Hey, close the window in there! (Goes to the mirror, looks at himself, examines his teeth, touches up his hair)

(Toilet flushes)

BRIGIT. If it rains we can go in Joe's car.

CHARLEY. Who said Joe was coming?

BRIGIT. I thought you said...he said he was coming...

CHARLEY. Did I said he said? Did I, did I? (Pulls her down onto the bed. They begin some heavy smooching which gets passionate. He reaches out from the bed

138

and puts on another record. Thunder outside)
Music...hath charms...to rrrrRRRRRRROUSE the
savage breast...

(BRIGIT has her T shirt off. He grabs her in a tight
embrace. She works his belt-buckle loose. They are
very excited. He tries to undo the top button of her
Levis and can't with one hand)

BRIGIT. (gasping) Let me...

(Undoes the button. CHARLEY undoes the zip and
thrusts his hand into her Levis. She moans and clutches
at him. Outside a car pulls up and beeps twice)

CHARLEY. (trying to untangle himself) Wait...

BRIGIT. (dizzy with passion) It's only Joe... (Tries to
hold CHARLEY down on her)

CHARLEY. (pulls away from her) Wait a minute... (Goes
to the window and whistles sharply)

BRIGIT. (panting furiously) God...you bastard!

JOE. (off) Hey hey!

CHARLEY. Hang on, I'll throw the key down!

JOE. Hey, man...am I interrupting anything?

CHARLEY. You're joking... (Throws the key) Come on up.

BRIGIT. (flushed, trembling) Would you like me to get
dressed?

CHARLEY. (raked by the contempt in her voice, avoids
looking at her) Suit yourself.

(BRIGIT simply slips down under the covers. Brilliant
flash of lightning outside and loud thunder. CHARLEY
puts on another LP and JOE comes in)

JOE. Hey, man!

(Lights a cigarette, wanders around the room.
CHARLEY does the same, JOE nods at the gram,
snaps his fingers at the music)

Nice...

CHARLEY. Fan-tastic.

JOE. You know the new Jimmy Brown?

CHARLEY. I heard it.

JOE. Better than Wilson Pickett... not the band, but him.

CHARLEY. Yeah?

BRIGIT. So where's Monika?

JOE. That new boutique... I've got to pick her up.

CHARLEY. What'd you do last night, then?

JOE. Pogo took us down to the Armpit. They have a new
show there. (Makes a slurping noise) Tits! Lots of
tits!

CHARLEY. (sniggering) I heard that wasn't all.

JOE. Yeah, well, they were going to do this thing, see...
they had this fantastic tart, she weighs about eighteen
stone... and they were going to do this thing with a
goat, you know? But someone told Jimmy the fuzz
were going to raid the place, and he chickened out.

CHARLEY. You sure it was Jimmy that chickened out, and
not the goat?

JOE. Eighteen stone, baby! Tits like lorry tyres! Anyway,
then we bumped into my brother. He took us out for
some drag racing. Man, that is out of sight! Our new
thing, you know?

CHARLEY. I thought your brother was always taking off
somewhere?

140

JOE. Yeah...he's getting really wild. He'll be all right.

CHARLEY. Sure, why not?

JOE. So where were you yesterday?

CHARLEY. We were...uh...hey, what'd we do yesterday?

BRIGIT. (sourly) We were here.

CHARLEY. No, we weren't...wait, that was the day before
...yeah, day before, we were at Pogo's.

JOE. What's Pogo up to?

CHARLEY. He's doing all right, I guess. His bird was
there. He's just...painting his pictures.

BRIGIT. Did Monika get back today?

JOE. Uh huh. This morning.

CHARLEY. So how are...things?

JOE. Oh, you know...the same...same shit. You writing
anything?

CHARLEY. Naah...not really.

JOE. What the hell is there to write? Man, I'm dried up...
just nothing...

(CHARLEY laughs)

JOE. You know, if we could write something...something
really wild, you know? Like...like we're talking
now, you know what I mean? Something like that...
really nice...or else...

CHARLEY. Right...right!

JOE. Listen...really now...what are we doing tonight?

CHARLEY. No idea.

JOE. No decent films on... anyway, I don't feel like a film...

BRIGIT. There's nothing on at all.

CHARLEY. Nah, I checked it all...nothing. Not even a shitty film.

BRIGIT. There's The Swedish Au Pair...nothing.

JOE. Hey man, did you see that one at the Rialto before?

CHARLEY. The Lash Cuts Deep?

JOE. About the nymphomaniac farm girl...

CHARLEY. And the masochistic horse...

JOE. Right! Right!

CHARLEY. I heard about it.

JOE. So... shall I come by later?

BRIGIT. You going already?

JOE. I've gotta pick up Monika.

BRIGIT. Anyway, come by...

CHARLEY. Or ring up...

(Thunder outside)

BRIGIT. Or we'll ring up.

JOE. No, I won't be home.

CHARLEY. Fine...okay, then...

JOE. Okay...I'll ring...

(But he doesn't leave. He and CHARLEY shuffle around)

JOE. Hey, what time is it?

CHARLEY. I dunno, my watch is...

 (Dials TIM and hands JOE the receiver)

JOE. (listening) Peep - peep - peep - (Drops the phone on the hook) Okay. So...do I come by? I mean, I don't mind, it's on the way.

BRIGIT. Come by.

JOE. Okay. I'll come by.

CHARLEY. Yeah, come by. Just in case.

JOE. Hey, are the parents back yet?

CHARLEY. Today or tomorrow. I dunno.

JOE. Too bad. We could have done something at the house.

CHARLEY. Yeah, well... (Shrugs)

JOE. Well, I'll come by...just in case.

CHARLEY. Right.

BRIGIT. Make sure we're in.

JOE. Yeah, I'll ring. Ciao.

CHARLEY. You don't have to ring. Just come by.

JOE. Yeah, okay. If anything exciting's happening.

CHARLEY. Just come by.

JOE. Okay, I will. Ciao. (Goes out)

CHARLEY. (calls after him) Hey, the key!

JOE. (off) I'll stick it in the post-box!

CHARLEY. Right!

(Goes to the window as another clap of thunder sounds. The car starts outside. Shouts down)

You don't have to ring, okay?

JOE. (off, through noise of motor) No, I'll come by!

CHARLEY. (closes the window) It's going to piss down all night. My God, the smoke in here!

BRIGIT. Let some air in!

(CHARLEY opens the window wide. The sound of rain outside. He puts another record on. BRIGIT crawls out of bed)

I'm going to take a shower.

(Goes out. The telephone rings)

CHARLEY. (picks up the receiver) Hel-lo...What? Who? Who am I? Why, lady, I'm the fucking Pope!

(Looks at the receiver, hangs up)

BRIGIT. (comes back in) Who was that?

CHARLEY. Wrong number.

BRIGIT. No hot water.

CHARLEY. Oh, no!

BRIGIT. Trickle, trickle...all gone.

(A long scene in dumbshow. Both of them loaf around the room reading or leafing through magazines, scanning record sleeves. A record plays softly. After a routine embrace by the bed they begin to dance. They laugh at each other maliciously. CHARLEY lolls out his tongue and tries to kiss her. She dodges and pokes him in the belly. They dance on, regarding each other through

half-closed eyes. They play elaborately at a jokey
hostility which is becoming genuine. CHARLEY aims
a light slap at her and she ripostes. He feigns injury,
dancing grotesquely, and she scratches the back of
flopping hand. He slaps her lightly but angrily. She
turns and wiggles her bum at him and he kicks her
lightly. She staggers, whirls and scratches him with
some force on the upper arm and they dance some
more, CHARLEY briefly inspecting his arm. He
dodges like a boxer larking about and then
suddenly gives her a ringing slap. She staggers back
and after a moment's shock, screams:)

BRIGIT. You cocksucker!

(She attacks him furiously, slapping, scratching. He
smothers her in bedclothes. She falls, grabs a bottle
and wings it at him, grazing him. CHARLEY puts on
a Wilson Pickett LP, and as she disentangles herself,
approaches her, smiling, and thumps her again. She
claws his face. He howls in pain and goes to the
mirror to inspect the deep scratches)

CHARLEY. Right.

(Now a real fight with BRIGIT screaming loudly and
CHARLEY swearing)

CHARLEY. You pig, you twat, you bloody little bitch, you
fucking cow, you cunt! (Matching epithets to blows,
he fells her with the last one) Now you crawl out of
here! Rub your fucking tits along the floor and fucking
crawl!

(Kicks her. She drags herself to the bed, sobbing convulsively. CHARLEY sits down and lights a cigarette,
trembling so badly that he drops it twice. N.B. This
fight must be long, harsh, loud and violent, including
pauses for panting, and end brutally)

CHARLEY. (pacing quickly up and down) What do you always
want to start scratching for? I told you last time that
if you scratched me again... (Pause) I don't even look
what I'm doing...I don't look...you get me?

145

BRIGIT. Give us a fag.

CHARLEY. (lights another cigarette, pats her on the back)
    There. (Gives her the cigarette over her shoulder)
    We'll take a walk, okay? (Goes to the window. The
    rain has stopped) Even if it does start to rain again.
    There it goes... (Rain outside. Pause) Fucking
    piss-arse weather.

    (BRIGIT gets up and begins to dress)

CHARLEY. What are you getting dressed for?

BRIGIT. (screams) Because I want to dress, you stupid
    arsehole!

CHARLEY. Okay... okay...

    (BRIGIT goes to the telephone and dials)

CHARLEY. I hope he's home...

BRIGIT. Get away...

CHARLEY. Who you calling, then?

BRIGIT. Hello... may I speak to Eddie, please? What...
    yes... yes... this is Brigit... when? I see. No,
    nothing special. No, it's not important. Just say I
    called to say hello. Yes... what? Oh, yes, please.
    (Pause) Yes, I'll wait.

CHARLEY. Isn't Eddie there? Is Eddie-teddie-weddie gone
    to beddie-bye? Without his sweetie-pie?

BRIGIT. (to CHARLEY) Oh, you'll see...

CHARLEY. Is he there?

BRIGIT. (pause) Hello? (Sweetly) Hi, Eddie! Fine,
    lovely. How are You? Yes... mmmm... oh, I'd like
    that...

CHARLEY. (loudly) He better pick you up from here right
    away!

146

BRIGIT. (covers the mouthpiece) Sorry, what?...What?

CHARLEY. (loudly) Next gentleman, please!

BRIGIT. No...of course not!

CHARLEY. Tell him he'd better pick you up right away!

BRIGIT. (to CHARLEY) Will you shut up? (To the telephone) No, not you. What?

CHARLEY. While you're still hot and wet!

BRIGIT. ...No...at Charley's place...yes...no!

CHARLEY. Because I'm going to kick your arse out of here!

BRIGIT. (angrily into the phone) Yes, at Charley's place. So? Oh, now, come on! But...look, are you coming or not?

CHARLEY. Tell him not to be such a prick!

BRIGIT. I know I haven't called for a long time...

CHARLEY. (childish nasal voice) Doesn' he WANNA come?

BRIGIT. (into the phone) Oh, God, you're so silly! No! No... no...no...you drive to the cemetery...you know... and then take the first left...

CHARLEY. Left into Rutland Avenue and the third house on the right...

BRIGIT. (into the phone) What? Oh, come on - what? Well, then don't! No...no, really, don't come!

CHARLEY. (yells) Jesus, what a twit! Take the first left after the ce-me-te-ry! God's garden suburb!

BRIGIT. (into the phone) What's that? All right! Fine. Fine. g'bye! I said, good...bye! (Slams down the receiver)

CHARLEY. So now fuck off.

147

BRIGIT. I'll just finish my cigarette.

CHARLEY. Okay. (Pause) I've <u>had</u> it with this bullshit of yours...right up to here.

BRIGIT. You can be bloody grateful you had me at all...

CHARLEY. Fuck<u>off</u>fuck<u>off</u>fuck<u>off</u>fuck<u>off</u>fuck<u>off</u>fuck<u>off</u>...

BRIGIT. Oh...<u>I</u> don't know what to do now...

CHARLEY. (pause) Don't you know some other git who has a car?

(BRIGIT smiles)

CHARLEY. Will you knock off the bullshit?

(BRIGIT laughs to herself)

CHARLEY. You hear me?

(BRIGIT laughs)

CHARLEY. So what are you laughing at?

BRIGIT. Nothing...

CHARLEY. What are you <u>laughing</u> at...

BRIGIT. It's so ridiculous...

CHARLEY. What?

BRIGIT. Me here with you...

CHARLEY. Your own fault.

BRIGIT. Hnh.

CHARLEY. Go on, just say you're here with me because I was your first... (Gesture)

(Pause)

BRIGIT. That's even more ridiculous...so...that's it...
finish...

CHARLEY. If you want to. I don't.

BRIGIT. Oh, sure. (Gets up) Let me out...

CHARLEY. You really want to go?

(Sound of JOE's Volkswagen outside)

BRIGIT. Is that Joe?

CHARLEY. (goes to the window) Yeah...

BRIGIT. Perfect...I can go with him...

CHARLEY. (whistles out the window, then takes BRIGIT by
the arm) Come on...out the back a second...come
on...

(He takes her out. After a moment MONIKA comes in.
She lights a cigarette and sits on the bed. Then she goes
out to the toilet. JOE comes in)

JOE. Monika?

MONIKA. (off) Just coming...

(JOE takes off his jacket, opens his shirt and pulls it
out of his pants, picks up a bottle, picks up a mashed
hat from the floor and puts it on, and regards himself
in the mirror. MONIKA comes back in)

MONIKA. Anything to drink?

JOE. Gin?

(Offers her the bottle)

MONIKA. Not for me.

JOE. You like my hat?

MONIKA. You look like the village idiot.

JOE. Try it...

MONIKA. Leave off...

JOE. (jams the hat down over her ears) Ha!

MONIKA. (rips off the hat and throws it away) Cretin.
(Pause) So where are they?

JOE. They wanted to go for a walk...

MONIKA. (Picks up a book, amused) Since when does
Charley read Wittgenstein?

JOE. He wants to improve his mind...anything wrong with
that? (Mockingly) It's beautiful to improve your mind...

MONIKA. Don't be so snotty...

JOE. Yeah, man...Wittgenstein... (Takes off his pants,
gets into bed, picks up a book)

MONIKA. When are they coming back?

JOE. Dunno.

MONIKA. Did Charley thump her?

JOE. Could be...

MONIKA. Just to show how masculine he is...

JOE. Uh huh...you ought to know...

MONIKA. He wasn't quite as floppy as you thought, either...

JOE. I hope not.

MONIKA. He was a little limp at first...but if I remember,
he was horny enough...in the end.

JOE. In the end? Oh, like that, was it? (No reaction from MONIKA) Put on some Wilson Pickett, hey...and slip into something more comfortable?

MONIKA. (Puts the LP on, strips off most of her clothes to the music and slips into bed with JOE) Very well, your Grace...away we gooo...

JOE. (nervous) A little hush, okay? Turn it up, please?

MONIKA. (lifts up the covers to look) Oh, my, we're not up at all, are we?

(JOE grabs down the covers. MONIKA smirks)

Don't be nervous now...no excuses...do it now or neverrr...

(Pause. Then cuttingly:)

Oooo, ba...beee...poochiewoochie teddy-bear can come and get his sugar-puffs...ooooh, teddy isn't going to ravish me?

(She is still groping. JOE thumps her with his elbow to make her stop and move away)

Oooooo0OOOOooooo...bang bang goes the little teddy-bear...bang bang with his el-bow...is that all teddy-bear can bang bang with? Hmmm? Hmmm? Hmmmmm? (Gropes)

JOE. Wait a minute...suppose someone comes in?

(MONIKA scratches him)

JOE. Ow! (Pause. He grabs her breast) My God! Polystyrene!

(MONIKA grabs too, under the covers. JOE doubles up suddenly)

Owww, Christ!

(They begin to scuffle and fight, entangled in the bedclothes. The struggle gets rough)

Don't do that...

(Thumps MONIKA's head which is covered by the blanket)

MONIKA. (screams furiously) OWWWWWW! (Emerges with blood pouring from her nose) Oh...God...my nose...

JOE. Lemme see... (Tries to look, but she has her hands over her face) Wait, get your hands away...get your hands away...

MONIKA. You son of a bitch...

JOE. Hey, you think it's broken? (She sobs. He reaches out and touches the nose. She screams loudly) Yep... broken, all right.

MONIKA. Take me to the doctor...right now!

JOE. Right, right...I couldn't really see what I was doing, see... (Paces, nervous and angry) Come on, get something on...

MONIKA. Oooohhhh...God... (Moans and sobs)

JOE. Does it hurt there, too?

MONIKA. Yes, it hurts...give me my blouse...

JOE. I better take you to the hospital...

MONIKA. Not the accident hospital...I'll have to wait... oh...God...

JOE. No, no the City Hospital...the casualty department... (Hesitates as she sobs) Hey, maybe I better ring up first...

MONIKA. All right...ring...damn...

JOE. Or maybe...maybe we should just go down there...
no, I better ring up...

MONIKA. Ring up, you silly bastard! Make sure the
doctor's there!

JOE. The doctor's there...I mean, it's a hospital...they've
got all kinds of doctors there...we'll just go...

MONIKA. Ring...up! (Grabs the telephone) At least look
up the number, if you're too stupid to ring up! (JOE
riffles in the phone book) It's the City Hospital.

JOE. All right, all right...what do you think I'm looking
up, the Police?

MONIKA. You can look them up, too.

JOE. (looks at her) Yeah, well...how do we say it happened?

MONIKA. Will you find the number?

JOE. Wait...City...Hospital...

MONIKA. Give me the number...

JOE. 859-2822 (MONIKA dials) But don't say how it happened...

MONIKA. Casualty department, please...a broken nose...
yes...a smashed nose... (Sobs)

JOE. Come on, we'll drive down...there'll be a doctor there...
come on... (MONIKA slams the phone down, stands
up) ...it'll be all right, babe... (Puts out his cigarette)

MONIKA. Let's go now, then!

(A whistle from outside in the street)

JOE. Hang on, I'll see who it is... (Goes to the window and
whistles)

CHARLEY. (outside) Joe?

JOE. Hey, man!

CHARLEY. Wanna go for a beer?

JOE. Not now, man...we got...just a second, I'll come down...

MONIKA. Go on!

CHARLEY. What is it?

JOE. Monika's nose is broken...

CHARLEY. Her nose is broken?

JOE. Right...we've gotta get down to the casualty department... hang on... (Quickly crosses the room) Let's go, come on...

(They go out and down the stairs, we hear them meet the others and exchange a few muffled words)

CHARLEY. (enters) Jesus, look at all the blood! (BRIGIT comes in) They're out of their minds...

BRIGIT. (mildly excited) I had no idea that Joe was such a ...brute!

CHARLEY. He said he didn't mean to...it was an accident ...you know...zap...before you even know what happens...boom...I can just imagine...

BRIGIT. Three cheers...

CHARLEY. You like it? I can do it too.

(BRIGIT laughs. CHARLEY pinches her from behind)

You don't think so? (Pinches her hard) You don't think so? (Kicks her half hard on the bottom, laughs as she slaps him)

BRIGIT. I just wish I knew what I saw in you.

CHARLEY. (pokes her in the breast) Not a thing...but...

154

you fancy me. Madly. (Boxes around her casually)
You fancy me madly... (Keeps boxing)

BRIGIT. Will you stop it?

(He boxes harder, she scratches him, he hits her,
she falls on the bed, throws a book at him, he throws
a book back and the ensuing book-fight becomes
increasingly light-hearted)

BRIGIT. (throws a book) Shitgenstein...

CHARLEY. (ripostes) Harold Pinter-shit!

BOTH. (ad lib, hurling books back and forth) Scott
Fitzgerald-shit, Edward Albee-shit, D.H. Lawrence-
shit, Tennessee Williams-shit, Sigmund Freud-shit,
William Burroughs-shit, William Shakespeare-shit,
Dostoyevsky-shit, Ronald Laing-shit, Henry Miller-
shit, Edward Bond-shit, Wilhelm Reich-shit, Arthur
Miller-shit, Gertrude Stein-shit, Jean Genet-shit,
Norman Mailer-shit, Samuel Beckett-shit, Bertrand
Russell-shit, C.G. Jung-shit, Jean-Paul Sartre-shit
Marshall McLuhan-shit, John Osborne-shit, William
Faulkner-shit, Ernest Hemingway-shit, Holy Bible-
shit, etc., etc., etc.

(In high spirits, but not affectionately, they stand laughing
at each other across the chaotic room. CHARLEY
puts on a loud record, conducts with both arms,
lurching among the rubbish, kicking things around)

CHARLEY. Ba-badoob-mbee-baaa...hey...hey...

BRIGIT. (shouting through the music) Charley. Charley!
Can't we tidy up this mess?

CHARLEY. (flings the bedclothes on the floor) You're
putting me on...

(Both of them smoke, moving around the room,
steamed up, nervous. Not a word is spoken)

CHARLEY. Any booze left?

BRIGIT. Some gin, I think...

CHARLEY. Bring it out! Man...I want to get smashed...
man, I'm...I dunno...

BRIGIT. You're what? Up tight?

CHARLEY. Yeah...up tight...but wild, you know? I can
feel all my nerves, you know? All together...
vibrating...get the gin, sweetie...

(BRIGIT goes out. CHARLEY hops grotesquely to
the music, falls heavily, howls, smothering the cry
in the bedclothes)

Bring a glass!

BRIGIT. (enters with bottle and glass) There.

CHARLEY. You have one too...

BRIGIT. There's some champagne out there...I thought
maybe you were saving it...

CHARLEY. Saving bullshit! Drink it! Drink it all!

(BRIGIT goes out for the champagne. CHARLEY
guzzles the gin)

BRIGIT. (brings in the champagne) Will you open it?
(CHARLEY gives her a friendly kiss, slips behind her
and pops the cork at her bum. She ignores it, smoking
calmly. CHARLEY gives her back the bottle) Is Joe
coming back?

CHARLEY. I guess so...not Monika, though, that's for sure...

BRIGIT. Then he should be here pretty soon...

CHARLEY. Uh huuuuh... (Paces up and down) Hey, what
do you say...we have a...suicide pact?

BRIGIT. Not for me. But you go right ahead.

CHARLEY. C'mon...we'll slide into a nice, hot bath,
right? And open up each other's arteries...right?
Kkkkkkkkk! See, you slide into a nice, hot bath...
because it doesn't hurt that way, right? I mean, I
read about it...and then you sssslice 'em open...
kkkkkkkkkk!

BRIGIT. Come on, Charley...let's tidy up...

CHARLEY. 'D I ever tell you about how Conrad wanted to
manufacture Teddy?

BRIGIT. (wearily) No...

CHARLEY. Man...what a groovy story that was...I could
even write a play about it...you know Teddy, right?

BRIGIT. The painter?

CHARLEY. Uh huh. You know he used to make umbrellas?
Hey. Pale-faced son of a bitch...and Conrad and this
other guy saw him one day down in the Art Club...and
all of a sudden Conrad says...you know what? We're
gonna manufacture him...

BRIGIT. What?

CHARLEY. Manufacture, see...really do it...he was going
to manufacture Teddy into a big deal artist, see...
everything...work it all out so he was gonna be famous,
right?...Then when they had him all made up, this
fantastic product, you know, famous and all that shit
...they were gonna fix it so he kkkkkkkk...farewell
cruel world, right?...But what happened, see...
Teddy didn't do it...Conrad did it... (Makes hanging
gesture, tongue out) kkkkkk! Isn't that wild? Not
Teddy...Conrad!

BRIGIT. Uh huh.

CHARLEY. I mean, someone's gotta do it, right? That's
the law of nature, ...sort of like...the sorcerer's
apprentice, right? ...so now Teddy is a big deal
famous artist...groovy character...that's the...law

157

of nature, right? Two groovy characters...and the grooviest character wins...all bullshit...all nerves and bullshit. (Goes to the window) Rain didn't cool it off...sultry out there...like a jungle...in here, too ...real Tennessee Williams atmosphere...hey, hey!

BRIGIT. Ha, ha.

CHARLEY. One more shitty afternoon...

BRIGIT. Don't keep talking like that...if you could just for once try to...

CHARLEY. Shitty...but intense...

BRIGIT. That's not what I mean by intense...you always think everything you do is intense...

CHARLEY. So what? (Pause) God, you are so...thick... sooooo fucking thick...I wish to Christ Joe would get back...

BRIGIT. Your sweet Joey-boy...you'd be lost without him, wouldn't you?

CHARLEY. I'd rather marry him than you.

BRIGIT. (laughs, embarrassed) Me, too.

CHARLEY. I just don't fancy you any more...all of a sudden I just don't fancy you any more...

BRIGIT. You think I fancy you?

CHARLEY. That's the tragedy of it...you do fancy me... you fancy me like a dog fancies a bone...you fancy me like mad...ah, ha...so I don't fancy you any more...

BRIGIT. That's all right with me. We can break it off...

CHARLEY. Break it off, break it off...how many times have I heard that shit...ah, ha...I don't wanna break it off and you're not gonna break it off...'s a very delicate distinction...an' you know that I need you...

yeah...I'll be glad when I can get away out of here...
best thing is to piss off right this minute...go to
Formentera, see Carla...

BRIGIT. What's the matter with you all of a sudden?

CHARLEY. (mocks her tone) Matter? What the hell d'you
think's the matter?

BRIGIT. Well, what?

CHARLEY. (pretty drunk) Yeah...today was just a little
bit too much...doesn' matter, though...Carla is at
least a...an agreeable person...hardly even speaks
English...doesn't bullshit all the time...just...
agreeable...you dig? ...agreeable...an agreeable
woman...no ulterior motives...you dig? ...she's just...
there...doesn' do anything...an' that's what makes
her perfect...anyway, she's fucking sexy...Christ, it
was great...full of hash in the burning heat...sweating
like a bloody fucking...stallion... (Takes a quick turn
around the room) You can piss off any time you want
to...

BRIGIT. Okay... (Gets up) Joe can take me home...

CHARLEY. If he does..if he does, that's fine...

BRIGIT. (goes to CHARLEY, kisses him tenderly) My
stupid baby...

CHARLEY. (smiles, backs away a bit) Oh yeah...oh, yeah
...women...women really have it hard...they really
do have it hard...

BRIGIT. You can say that again...

CHARLEY. I was just discussing that very thing with
Freddy...

BRIGIT. With Freddy...

CHARLEY. And he is also of the opinion...that women
really do have it very hard...

BRIGIT. (grabs him) Why are you so nasty all of a sudden?

CHARLEY. I told you how nasty I can get...just like that...
and now...I'm nasty...and it feels great!

(Makes provocative movements. JOE's Volkswagen is
heard)

BRIGIT. There's Joe. I'll go down right now.

CHARLEY. Right, piss off...

BRIGIT. Are any of my things here?

CHARLEY. I dunno...

BRIGIT. (rummaging around) What?

CHARLEY. Out of it... (Bellows suddenly:) Piss off, damn
you! Fuck off out of it! Aren't you gone yet?

(BRIGIT throws herself on the bed and weeps. CHARLEY
puts on Sergeant Pepper's Lonely Hearts Club Band.
JOE enters)

CHARLEY. Hey, man...drink up! (Gives him the bottle)

JOE. (takes it and drinks, nodding at BRIGIT) What's up
with her?

CHARLEY. Who knows, man...so what's new?

JOE. Nothing new, man...you know what happened...

CHARLEY. Broken nose...

JOE   Right...

CHARLEY. So? They didn't keep her in the hospital?

JOE. (tragic pose) Yes! (Pause) My poor love...
(Smiles cynically but keeps the same tragic tone)
My lovelovelovelovelovelovelovelovelooooove...

CHARLEY. Yeah, man...not so simple...motherfucker...
love...

JOE. (sings to the record) Sergeant Pepper's Lonely Hearts
Club Band...man, when you think...when you think...
there's one thing, man...there's just one thing that's
really dangerous...really dangerous, you dig?...
and that...is re-pro-fucktion...you dig me, man?

CHARLEY. I dig.

JOE. I dunno...I dunno...man, I am so thirsty...

CHARLEY. Drink up! (BRIGIT sobs. He speaks to her in
a friendly tone:) Will you belt up? Come on, have
some gin... (Yells louder) HEY!

JOE. Hey, man...I got some stuff...if you wanna turn on...

CHARLEY. Who from?

JOE. Sonny gave it to me before he took off...

CHARLEY. Good stuff?

JOE. I made a joint with it last week...beautiful...not like
that shit the time before...

CHARLEY. Let's roll one, man...

JOE. You wanna do it?

CHARLEY. Right... (To BRIGIT, who is still on the bed)
Hey, you got your nail scissors? (She does not answer.
JOE takes out the hash and cigarettes, and papers.
CHARLEY speaks to JOE:) Hang on, I'll get some
scissors...

JOE. (to BRIGIT) You gonna smoke? (No reply)

CHARLEY. (brings in the scissors) It couldn't be a better
day for it.

JOE. Man, we're half-way stoned already...

161

CHARLEY. (finishing the first joint) Looks good, man, looks good...

JOE. (slopes around the room, keeping time on his own head) Right there...papapapapa...tatatapapa tatam! Tatam...ttm... (Drums on the edge of a table... faster and faster)

CHARLEY. Ehy, we've got to put on something really groovy ... (JOE drums away) Hey, put something on...

JOE. Right...

CHARLEY. Which one?

JOE. The Stones...something cool...

(Puts on Back Street Girl. The cigarette is ready. In the stillness BRIGIT sits up on the bed and watches them with tear-filled eyes)

JOE. Go ahead, man...

CHARLEY. Right...matches...matches...

JOE. There...

CHARLEY. (before he lights up) You know Val got busted?

JOE. Yeah, I heard...up at Pete's place...they got everybody...

CHARLEY. Yeah, well, they were all stoned out of their minds...the fuzz were in before they knew what was happening...they got Danny too...poor fucker was on shit...he flipped, he just flipped... (Lights up, inhales deeply) Beautiful, man...beautiful... (Draws deep again, passes the joint to JOE, who also takes two deep drags. They smile at each other. The gram is turned up. Both rise and wander around. BRIGIT lights a cigarette and leans back. CHARLEY goes to the window) Wait, I'll close the window. (Closes the shutters, then the window, turns on the light and laughs to JOE)

162

JOE. You rolled a strong one, man...

CHARLEY. Right...plenty more where that came from...
(They pace, heads down. BRIGIT turns down the
music)

CHARLEY. (gradually turning on) Beautiful...beautiful...
out of sight...

JOE. Really out of sight...nothing wrong with this stuff,
man...

CHARLEY. Wrooooong...he-heyyy...

JOE. Ga-dong dong...doooooong...

(Both laugh briefly, then get hold of themselves and
keep their cool. They move up and down, making
slightly grotesque movements to the music, seeming
gay but not really high. Cheerfully they smoke the
cigarette to the end)

CHARLEY. (to BRIGIT) Come on, try it...

BRIGIT. Joe can drive me home now...

JOE. Since when am I a taxi?

CHARLEY. Oh...madame...   (Bows low) The fucking
underground is at your service...

BRIGIT. (lies down again, weeps) You mean bastards!

CHARLEY. This is groovy stuff...

JOE. Sonny got it really cheap...

CHARLEY. Where?

JOE. Dunno...a kayf in Istanbul or...somewhere in Turkey,
I dunno...he's living off it now...

CHARLEY. Hey, that's beautiful...for an insurance man...

JOE. Not now, man...he switched...didn't like the office

163

any more...didn't like that old death insurance...so he switched to happy life insurance, dig?

CHARLEY. (laughs wildly) Happy...happyyyy...hey, hey! Happy <u>all</u> the <u>time</u>... (Laughs)

JOE. (takes it up) Happy <u>happy</u> hap hap...ba-dap zap...ba-dap ...<u>ba-dap</u>...bap-ydap...happyyyyy...

CHARLEY. (does a kind of horsey dance around the room to the music) Ba-dap-y-<u>dap</u> giddyyap...giddyap...bap bap...badapydappy dap <u>dap</u>py dap lappy lap <u>lap</u> hapalappy lap lap... (Collapses in helpless laughter)

JOE. (rolling another joint) Nice walkies...nice horsie take a nice walkie talkies...

CHARLEY. (dancing) Happy <u>all</u> the time...ba-dime dime... be-dime diiiime... (Stumbles, falls)

JOE. Pigeon in the grass on your arse arse arse... (Lights the joint) OOooooooo eeeeeeeeee...ba-doom doooooom...

CHARLEY. (gets up to take the joint) Boom boom boom... (Deep drag) boomy doom <u>doooooooom</u>! (Pirouettes, letting out the smoke slowly)

JOE. Mooom...mooom...muuuusic...'sgoing on forever... man...music's going on and on...and on...

CHARLEY. A-go <u>bye</u>...bye...

JOE. I know <u>why</u>...why...

CHARLEY. Cause we're <u>high</u>...high...

JOE. A-know <u>why</u>...high...

CHARLEY. <u>Die</u>...die...

BOTH. Higher...higher...higher...higher... (Dancing wildly, singing the words ad lib, but with strong rhythm, they whirl to the music, keeping time wildly, giggling, swooping at last to a staggering stop on either side of the bed where BRIGIT lies)

CHARLEY. (bends over unsteadily, pulls up the hem of

BRIGIT's T-shirt to peer underneath. She slaps his
hand away. CHARLEY wags his finger at JOE) Very
short skirt...

JOE. That skirt...is a T...shirt!

CHARLEY. T...shirt, see shirt!

JOE. Me shirt, Bee shirt...

CHARLEY. Pretty shirt shirt...

JOE. Titty shirt shirt... (Makes an unsteady try at
BRIGIT's bust. She rolls onto her stomach)

CHARLEY. Shirty shirt shirt...

JOE. (catching the rhythm) Shitty shirt shirt...

CHARLEY. (pointing to BRIGIT's bum and silently clapping
his hands) Shitty shirt, shitty shirt, shitty shirt shirt...

BOTH. (pounding the rhythm on BRIGIT's bum, JOE with one
hand, the other holding the joint out of harm's way)
Shitty shirt, shitty shirt, shitty shirt shirt...

BRIGIT. (screams) Stop it! (Turns and kicks, but they
stagger back out of range)

CHARLEY. (snapping fingers in rhythm) Well, buzz, buzz,
cuz...here come de fuzz...

JOE. (same rhythm) Yes he does...yes, he does...

CHARLEY. ...fuzz fuzz cuz...buzz buzz buzz...

JOE. Fuzzl buzzl muzzl cuzzl, ...

CHARLEY. Duddy duzz duzz...cuzz, cuzz? Uzz? Uzz?

JOE. (pointing at BRIGIT, who has again rolled onto her
stomach) Guzz, guzz!

CHARLEY. (nodding cheerfully) Duzz duzz!

BOTH. (holding BRIGIT down and pounding her bum again
in rhythm) Buzz, buzz, here come de fuzz, duzz cuzz
buzz? Duzz he duzz! Fuzzl buzzl wuzzl cuzzl, duzzee
duzz duzz! Guzz, cuzz, here come de fuzz! Here
come de fuzz! Duzz duzz duzz! Fuzz fuzz fuzz! Duzz
duzz duzz...

(BRIGIT kicks, screams and they can't hold her. They
stagger back and bawl in chorus, ignoring the record:
singing)

We come from Ro-dean,
    nice girls are weeeee...
We haven't lost our
    vir-gin-ityyyyy...

(They break into camp shrieks and giggles, flopping
about, then, arms around each other's waist, bawl
another song:)

Sheeeeeeeeeee...
hasn't a spot on her character, no,
she hasn't a spot on her name...
she lives in a spot
not far from the spot
the spot that's called spottery lane...
Sheeeeeeeeeee's...
got spots on her fingers and spots on her toes,
and spots on the end of her nose...
but the most charming spot
is the spot that she's got
the spot on the end of her
    toora-lye, tooralye, oora-lye...ayyyyye...

(Now they howl war-cries and shuffle around in the
rubbish grunting the nonsense in Indian rhythms)

Buzz, buzz, buzz, buzz, fuzz, uzz, uzz, uzz, fuzz
buzz, fuzz buzz, duzz, uzz, uzz, uzz, here come de
fuzz, here come de fuzz, here come de fuzz, de fuzz
duzz duzz, fuzzl duzzl duzzl duzzl...

JOE. (wiggling index finger in his mouth, utters a loud war-
cry, then burbles like an idiot) b-b-b-b-b-b-b-b-b-b

...g-g-g-g-g-g-g-g-g-g...b-b-b-b-b-b-b-beautiful
...beautifoooooooooool...

CHARLEY. Beautiful, cutieful...suitiful...dutiful...

JOE. Easy Rider...dieder...slider...

CHARLEY. (pulling eyes into slants, bowing, with Jap
     accent) Ah, soo...you ah supprize I spik you rangradge...

JOE. (pointing to CHARLEY, lisping) D'you love me?

CHARLEY. Kick him in the knee!

JOE. (camply furious) You love the dolls!

CHARLEY. Kick him in the other knee!

JOE. Muuuuuusic...muuuusic...

CHARLEY. It's a trick, man, a tricky trick trick...

JOE. Sicky sick trick trick...

CHARLEY. Cha cha cha, sick sick,

JOE. Chachacha, prick prick,

BOTH. Chachacha dick dick, chachacha sick sick, chachacha
     lick, lick, chachacha prick prick, hahaha dick dick,
     chachacha chick chick, (Very loud, rising to a climax)
     gagaga nick, nick, chachacha sick sick, chacha chow
     dick, dick, wowowow ick ick, wowowow, wowowow
     WOWOWOW WOWOWOW... (Both reeling, staggering,
     yelling, laughing hysterically. They face each other
     with open arms)

JOE. Old darling!

CHARLEY. Old fruit!

     (They embrace and kiss each other deeply on the
     mouth. BRIGIT runs into the kitchen)

JOE. Wass the matter with her? Doesn't like to see the
      fellas kiss...fellas are beautiful...beautiful thing in
      the whoooooole world...

CHARLEY. Beautifuller than the...beautiful... (Takes a
      globe out of the wardrobe, takes the sphere out of its
      frame, and throws it to JOE) Catch!

JOE. The world...is really...all...fucked up... (They
      both gape silently at the globe)

CHARLEY. (dreamily) S' beautiful...

JOE. Ah, you're flipped!

CHARLEY. Look man...beauuuuutiful...

JOE. I think...I think...I'm gonna trash this world...right
      down the shit-hole...with all the other shit...

CHARLEY. (holding his nose, speaking as though he had a
      cold) The pladet (planet) has had it...how sad it will
      be...and now we will bury it down in the seeeeeeaa..

      (They troop gaily out with the globe)

JOE. (outside in the bog) Byyyyyyeee world!

CHARLEY. (softer) Bye - eye... (There is a splash, then
      the flushing of the toilet) It won't goooo! (Chants)
      The world is moving on the face of the waaa...terrs...

JOE. It won't go...

CHARLEY. (chants) As it was in the beginning...

JOE. (chants) ...is now...

CHARLEY. (chants) ...and ever shaaalll beeeee...ha, ha!

JOE. (chants) ...shaaall beeee...ha, ha!

BOTH. (chanting) Shaaalll beee, ha, ha! Shaaalll beee, ha,
      ha! Shaaalll beee, ha, ha! Shaaalll beee, ha, ha!

(They laugh and come back in)

CHARLEY. I'm...observing myself again...when I get
    stoned...I'm always observing myself...

JOE. It's a stake-out, man!

CHARLEY. Buzz, buzz, here come de fuzz... (Giggles)

JOE. Man, that record is so slooow...sooo slooooww...

CHARLEY. You just wanna stand...dig? ...just stand for
    a while, right there...don' dance! ...an' then...
    after while...then you flip around... (Pirouettes)
    like this... (Holds a grotesque pose) that's the new
    thing, man!

JOE. Where're those comic books, man? I wanna look at
    that groovy one...

CHARLEY. Zap? Mister Natural? Yellow Dog?

JOE. No, man...that other one...what was it?

CHARLEY. Captain Guts? Little Johnny Fuckerfaster?

JOE. There was this little creep in it, with the gigantic
    cock...

CHARLEY. Old Uncle Uh-Uh and His Garbage Truck...

JOE. Not that one..he just blew this bird right apart, man
    ...her eyes popped out and everything...out of sight...

CHARLEY. That was Skull Comics, man...no, Racist Pig
    Comics...

JOE. No, I know what it was...it was Fat Lip Funnies.

CHARLEY. Ohhh, man...I'm sorry...Louie took it last
    week. The fucker never brought it back...

JOE. What's this one like? Elephant Doodie?

CHARLEY. Nah, Wee-Wee Comics is better. Or Meatball.
Look at this...Harry Kirschner...or Clumpy Morphus...

JOE. (picking up another one) ...too much...Granny Crack-Baggy?

BRIGIT. (comes in again) Why don't you both just piss off?

CHARLEY. (gapes at her, then to JOE) Wassat? You seen
that before?

JOE. Man...I never seen that before...

CHARLEY. (laughs) Wassat...'f anybody pisses off, you
piss off...your presence here...is...uncalled for...

JOE. Un-called for...nun-called-for...balled for...

CHARLEY. Your...type is not called for...at the moment
...you are an un-called-for...type!

JOE. Don't call us...we'll call you...

BRIGIT. You shut up! Suppose I call the police and tell
them you've got hash up here?

(Both men explode into laughter)

JOE. Buzz buzz...here come de fuzz...fuzzl wuzzl cuzzl...

CHARLEY. Buzza Buzza Buzza...here-a come-a fuzza...
fuzz...l fuzz...l... (Calling) Haul in the fore-sail...

JOE. Land hoooooooo!

CHARLEY. Hey...roll another one...

JOE. Right...one more for the hiiiiigh road...once more
with feeling... (Rips apart a cigarette for the tobacco,
mixes in the hash, rolls it up in a paper) I could stick it do
it down in the cigarette, man, but this is quicker...
strong this time, man...really strong...right? Hang
on...just a second...beautiful...beautiful... (JOE
lights up, BRIGIT grabs the joint and flings it away.

CHARLEY picks it up)

CHARLEY. Still alive, man... (Lights it if necessary, if not, puffs ecstatically)

JOE. (to BRIGIT) You flipped? What's the matter with you? Cunt!

(BRIGIT slaps him)

CHARLEY. You're flipping out!

BRIGIT. You're the ones who are flipping out! (Tries to open the window) Fucking hash-heads...

CHARLEY. Ah-ah-ah-ah-...that stays shut... (Stops her) That just stays shut...

BRIGIT. I can't breathe in here!

CHARLEY. Then fuck off!

BRIGIT. All right... (Goes to the telephone, dials a number)

JOE. (sings) Ah'm gonna getcha on the tel-e-phone... Ain't never gonna letcha be a-lone...

BRIGIT. Will you shut up?

JOE. (nasal voice) What is your number, please? May I have your number, please?

CHARLEY. Darling! I love you!

JOE. No! Think of Cynthia! (Picks up a Playboy and opens the gatefold)

CHARLEY. (tragically covering his eyes) She knows! Everything!

JOE. (back of fist against forehead) No! My God! No!

BRIGIT. Hello?

CHARLEY. I tell you she knows! She knows!

JOE. Aaaaaaaaaaaggggghhh! (Falls on his face)

BRIGIT. Hello? (To the others) Will you please shut up?

(Both of them, grunting their buzz-fuzz Indian rhythm,
dance in a circle. BRIGIT hangs up and dials another
number)

JOE. Man, I'm blowing my mind... flying, man, flying...

CHARLEY. Moi aussi...

(They imitate planes, buzzing BRIGIT. Then a silence
falls)

JOE. (picks up a newspaper, rolls it into a long cylinder,
moans) Cynthia, Cynthia, I can't get you out of my
mind! (Holds the cylinder like an erect penis)

CHARLEY. Forget her... you mad fool!

JOE. I'll try, by God, I'll try! (The newspaper cylinder,
which he has held erect, now droops)

CHARLEY. That's the way! That's the way! (Erects his
own cylinder)

JOE. You bloody swine! You want her!

CHARLEY. You, my darling! I want you!

BRIGIT. (hangs up, dials another number) You bastards
think you're only playing.

CHARLEY. (gets the bolster from the bed, holds it at his
crotch) Likey likey... nice lady fucky fucky?

BRIGIT. Piss off!

JOE. Ooom ooom, baby... ooom ooom...

CHARLEY. Hare krishna... oom oom... hare hare... oom...

JOE. Nice lady...nice lady...oom...oom...

CHARLEY. Nice lady jigajig...fucky fucky?

>   (They crowd close to BRIGIT, who is having no
>   success w th the phone)

BRIGIT. Fuck off!

CHARLEY. Suck off? Sweet heart!

>   (BRIGIT knees him in the crotch. He doubles up and
>   rolls on the floor)`

BRIGIT. (mincing voice) Oooooo...does it hurt?

>   (JOE comes forward with a chair like a lion tamer,
>   pushing BRIGIT)

BRIGIT. Stop it!

JOE. (pushing harder) Back, boy, back!

BRIGIT. Stop it, I said! (Takes hold of the chair and pushes
back)

>   (CHARLEY puts on another record, fairly loud, then
>   takes the bolster and holds it in front of his crotch
>   again. He and JOE begin to dance around BRIGIT,
>   each wielding his respective weapon. JOE takes off
>   his shirt, CHARLEY does the same)

CHARLEY. (to BRIGIT, who has left the phone) C'mon, you
too...

JOE. Strip off...we'll all strip off...

>   (They keep dancing)

CHARLEY. You won't strip off?

JOE. I'm flying, man...flying out of sight...

BRIGIT. You start...

CHARLEY. (thumps her with the bolster, falls down himself)
Wooomp!

JOE. (tries to open BRIGIT's zipper, half succeeds) Hey,
that zipper sounds like my motor...wild...wild...
wild!

CHARLEY. (also tries, pulls the Levis down a little)
Verrr-y sexy...

BRIGIT. (pulls up the Levis, goes for CHARLEY, who runs
away, giggling like a little girl) Chickenshit! (JOE
shoves her with the chair from behind, she goes for
him in turn, and he runs away giggling. CHARLEY
gooses her with the champagne bottle) Damn you!

(She throws something at his head, as JOE tries to
get her Levis down again. She shoves him away, he
falls on the bed and she is about to thump him when
CHARLEY shoves her onto the bed. All three jump
up again. She throws herself at JOE but falls on the
floor and he jumps on her)

CHARLEY. Gotcha!

JOE. (holding her hands behind her back, in a high voice:)
Police! Police! Police!

CHARLEY. Release, release, release! (BRIGIT gets up)
And now...strip off! (She grabs her bag and makes a
dash for the door, but he is there first, blocking the
way, crooning in a Mexican accent:) Hey, leetle
gor-orl, I want to show you some-theeng...

BRIGIT. Fuck off! (Tries to force him out of the way)

JOE. Hey leetle gor-orl...we love you... (Grabs her breasts
from behind. She twists away from him, kicking and
missing, tearful with fury)

CHARLEY. (struggles with her hand to hand, then pushes
her away, so that she stands between him and JOE)
Doooon't be afraaaiid, leetle gorl...

BRIGIT. (gasping and sobbing) You chickenshits...

JOE. (imitating a chicken) fuuuuuckfuckfuckfuckfuckfuckfuck...

CHARLEY. (wielding a jacket like a cape) Toro! Toro!

JOE. Huuuh! Huuuuuh! (Giggles. Both harry her, trying to get her to charge, using jackets like capes, grunting and shouting toro, toro ad lib. She dodges away from them and goes to the phone dialling)

CHARLEY. (pinches her from behind) Who are you cal-leeng, leetle gor-orl?

JOE. Buzz buzz the fuzz?

CHARLEY. Here come de fuzzluzzl?

JOE. (loudly) Toro!

BRIGIT. (jumps with fright. CHARLEY rips the receiver from her hand. There is a scuffle) I'll scream! (She screams, he lets her go. She tries the door again, but CHARLEY stops her)

CHARLEY. Huuuuh! Toro, toro!

JOE. I theenk the bool he ees not very brave, ami-go...

(BRIGIT is near hysterical)

CHARLEY. The bool I theenk he fancy me, amigo...

JOE. Also I theenk I'm fancying the bool...

(He has picked up a stool. Both make mooing and bleating noises, shoving BRIGIT one way and then the other, JOE with his stool and CHARLEY with the bolster. An extra hard shove from JOE's stool sends her reeling past CHARLEY to fall into the debris near the window. She comes up weeping hysterically and holding a kitchen knife)

JOE. Hey amigo...the bool he have one horn...

175

BRIGIT. (screams desperately) Get away from me! (Tries to make the door again, but is driven back unmercifully harrassed with pillows which the boys wield like muletas)

CHARLEY. Huuuh, huuuh, toro...toro...

JOE. Hey...toro! (Whacks her on the bum with his pillow)

CHARLEY. (as BRIGIT turns to face JOE, whacks her in turn with a pillow) Hey toro!

JOE. (repeating the trick) Toro, toro!

(They begin to pound her with the pillows, forgetting that she has the knife. The pounding increases in tempo as they laugh and shout to each other:)

CHARLEY. Hey, ami-go, the bool he ees cheecken...

JOE. He don' like to fight, I thee-eenk!

(Shouting, whooping, they close in on her, pounding with the pillows until the three of them are entangled in a general shoving, shouting pounding struggling melee. Suddenly BRIGIT's hysterical scream cuts through the yelling and uproar:)

BRIGIT. GET AWAY FROM MEEEEEEEEE!

(They all stumble together in a flurry of pillows and floundering confused arms and heads. JOE staggers b back with his face against the wardrobe while CHARLEY reels onto the bed, laughing helplessly. BRIGIT stands still, her hysteria suddenly gone, icily calm. She watches JOE)

CHARLEY. (doubled up) Hey amiiigo the bool he ees feenesh I theenk... (Something about BRIGIT makes him stop laughing and look at JOE. JOE turns from the wardrobe, not too slowly, moving convulsively. The knife protrudes from his chest and blood pours down the front of him, soaking all the front of his shirt and pants)

CHARLEY. (numb) No...

JOE. (staggers toward CHARLEY) Char...ley... (Sinks
down, dies at BRIGIT's feet)

CHARLEY. (still numb, plunges forward almost auto-
matically as JOE sinks, catches his hand. As he holds
the hand, BRIGIT sits calmly on the bed) Joe...Joe?
What'd you do? Joe? (Still numb, looks at BRIGIT)
What'd you do? ...You flipped...you flipped...no...
no, you flipped...I mean...what am I gonna do...I
mean... (Drops the hand in horror and stands up,
backing away) Is he dead? Hey, is he dead?
Hey, you think he's dead? (Watches dumbly as BRIGIT
goes to the phone, then decides not to call) He's dead...

BRIGIT. (icily) It was self-defence.

CHARLEY. Yeah...yeah, right...I mean...you flipped...
uh...uh...God, I...man, I'm still stoned...it's all...
all...I mean...what are you gonna do? I mean, you've
gotta do something...I mean, I'm...stoned, right?
what...what are we gonna do? ...Christ, what if
someone comes...can you look at him? Please?

BRIGIT. Stop it.

CHARLEY. He's dead...listen, baby, you...you flipped
your mind...you flipped your mind...listen, someone
might come...somebody might come...I mean, just
think if somebody comes...

BRIGIT. (goes to JOE, picks up his hand, feels for a pulse)
Yes, he's dead. (She is cool and calm)

CHARLEY. No...not really...listen, really? (Cringes in
a corner) Man, I'm...flipping out...I'm flipping out
...listen...what are we gonna do?

BRIGIT. (calmly) Nothing. It was self-defence. He tried
to rape me.

CHARLEY. I mean...I mean...I mean...you flipped...no!
(Disoriented, moves around. BRIGIT puts on Play

With Fire by the Stones, lights a cigarette)

CHARLEY. Hey, I...I feel funny...I feel really funny...
hey...turn down the record...please, turn down the
record...

BRIGIT. (warm, friendly) Come on...

CHARLEY. Listen, if somebody hears it...

BRIGIT. (removing her Levis and T-shirt) Come on...
(She is left wearing briefs)

CHARLEY. What...whatsa matter...what're you doing that
for?

(She turns down the lights, then lights a candle)

BRIGIT. (soft but excited) Come on... (Goes to him, opens
his shirt, pulling him toward the bed. Some afternoon
light comes through the closed shutters)

CHARLEY. (dazed) What're you doing...

BRIGIT. (voice thick with excitement) Don't you like me
any more? (Pulls him down onto the bed, tries to get
him to pull down the briefs)

CHARLEY. (whimpering) I can't do that... (Collapses on
his knees at the side of the bed, puts his head on her
knee, clutches at her leg like a child)

BRIGIT. (pushing him violently aside, stands up angrily
and turns on the light) Christ!

CHARLEY. (dreamily) We gonna go now?

(BRIGIT is calmly getting dressed again)

CHARLEY. (stumbles around the room, finds a small rug
and rolls JOE's body in it, then pulls it behind the bed)
Hey...you won't tell anybody we were smoking...you
know?... (Starts violently) Somebody coming...
(Plunges to the door) Didn't you hear...hey?...

BRIGIT. (takes the car key from JOE's jacket and goes to the door where CHARLEY cringes) Get out of the way. I'm going now.

CHARLEY. (clutches at her) Where you going?

BRIGIT. (pries his hands loose) Will you let go, please?

CHARLEY. (coming apart) No...don't go...I mean...they'll see you...I mean, they'll get you...wait...just wait'll I come down...

(BRIGIT coldly pushes him aside and goes)

CHARLEY. (as the door closes in his face) No, wait... wait...

(Too frightened to open the door, he stumbles back across the room, shambles about, finds himself staring down at the body. The car starts up outside, pulls away. He sits down, starts up in panic, listens at the door, goes to the window and listens, lurches to the wardrobe and climbs in, shutting the door. A pause. The phone rings. After five rings CHARLEY slinks out of the wardrobe and lifts the receiver without saying anything. Then he whispers:)

Who...oh...Monika... (Very softly) Joe? Uh...he left already...I dunno...you can't hear me? (Still softly) No, really...he's not here...maybe...he went to the movies... (Obviously wanting to end the conversation) Yeah...yeah, I'll tell him...yeah...yeah... right...bye... (Hangs up and tiptoes back to the wardrobe to shut himself in)

THE END

C AND B PLAYSCRIPTS

OTHER C AND B PLAYS

Adamov, Arthur	PAOLO PAOLI PING PONG and Professor Taranne
Antrobus, John	YOU'LL COME TO LOVE YOUR SPERM TEST (New Writers IV)
Arrabal, Fernando*	PLAYS VOLUME I (Orison, Fando and Lis, The Car Cemetery, The Two Executioners) PLAYS VOLUME II (Guernica, The Labyrinth, Picnic On the Battlefield, The Tricycle, The Condemned Man's Bicycle) PLAYS VOLUME III (The Grand Ceremonial, The Architect and Em- peror of Assyria, The Solemn Communion)
Borchert, Wolfgang	THE MAN OUTSIDE
Beckett, Samuel*	COME AND GO
Duras, Marguerite	THREE PLAYS (The Square, Days in the Trees, The Viaducts of Seine- et-Oise) THE RIVER AND THE FORESTS (In The Afternoon of Monsieur Andesmas)
Ionesco, Eugène*	PLAYS VOLUME I (The Chairs, The Bald Prima Donna, The Lesson, Jacques) PLAYS VOLUME II (Amédée, The New Tenant, Victims of Duty)

PLAYS VOLUME
III
(The Killer, Improvisation,
Maid to Marry)
PLAYS VOLUME
IV
(Rhinoceros, The Leader,
The Future Is in Eggs)
PLAYS VOLUME
V
(Exit the King, The Motor Show
Foursome)
PLAYS VOLUME
VI
(A Stroll in the Air,
Frenzy for Two)
PLAYS VOLUME
VII
(Hunger and Thirst,
The Picture, Anger,
Salutations)
PLAYS VOLUME
VIII
(We All Fall Down,
The Oversight)
PLAYS VOLUME
IX
(Macbett, The Vase,
Learning to Walk)
THREE PLAYS
(The Killers, The
Chairs, Maid to
Marry)
THE BALD PRIMA DONNA
(Typographic Edition)

Jupp, Kenneth   A CHELSEA
TRILOGY
(The Photographer,
The Tycoon,
The Explorer)

Mercer, David	THE GENERATIONS (Where the Difference Begins, A Climate of Fear, The Birth of a Private Man) THREE TV COMEDIES (A Suitable Case for Treatment, For Tea on Sunday, And Did Those Feet) THE PARACHUTE with Let's Murder Vivaldi, In Two Minds RIDE A COCK HORSE
Obaldia, René de*	PLAYS VOLUME I (Jenousia and Seven Impromptus for Leisure) PLAYS VOLUME II (The Satyr of La Villette, The Unknown General, Wide Open Spaces)
Pinget, Robert*	PLAYS VOLUME I (Clope, Dead Letter, The Old Tune) PLAYS VOLUME II (Architruc, About Mortin, The Hypothesis)
Walser, Martin	THE RABBIT RACE and THE DETOUR
Weiss, Peter	THE MARAT/SADE THE INVESTIGATION

* These Authors represented for dramatic presentation by
C and B (Theatre), 18 Brewer Street, London W1R 4AS